Doubting Thomas

By

Thomas Healy

DOUBTING THOMAS

Dedication

This book is a dedication to Mary Healy.

About the Author

I met Thomas about 20 years ago at the Edinburgh Book Festival. He was a tall man in his fifties, quietly spoken, and there was a mutual attraction between us. At this meeting, I could never have guessed what an unusual, adventurous life he had led. He was a bachelor and never wanted to be tied or make commitments, but he loved casual romances. He himself said that he had always been too fond of the lassies. He told me that he was born in the Gorbals and lived with his mother, father, and his sister Mary. He was surrounded by Irish relatives and remembers his granny as an old witchlike woman, dressed in black, smoking her clay pipe, with her kitchen always full of visiting Irish cronies.

Thomas had a happy childhood playing in the streets and going for his weekly visit on a Saturday morning to the Ritz Cinema with Mary and his friend William. He said himself that he was the dunce of his class but was very popular and excelled in all sports and became captain of the school football team. A turning point in his life came when coming back from playing football, elated, as he had just been selected to go for a trial for the Scottish youth team; he was met with the news that his father had died of a massive heart attack aged 46 years.

Thomas never played football again and never went to the trials. His mother and sister were distraught, and his home became a house of mourning. He had become very close to his father in the last year as he had changed bedrooms and now shared with his father and Mary with her mother.

At night his father would regale him with stories of his time in the army, how he had been their champion boxer, and his holidays to Galway as a boy. In the last years of his life, he became very religious. He insisted that the family say the Rosary every evening, with Mary and Thomas secretly making funny faces at each other.

Now, after his death, Thomas roamed the streets at night with no discipline, and he was lucky he avoided the gangs and spent his time frequenting boxing gyms. After his father's death, his mother got a job as a dinner lady. From then on, the food was plentiful as she could bring the leftovers home. Sometimes, when the electricity bill was unpaid, his mother sent them to the chapel, and the priest gave them some candles, which they loved when sitting at night in their candlelit kitchen, but his mother was ashamed that the neighbors would notice. Thomas always said that his father's death changed his life's direction.

PROLOGUE

That Christmas Eve, we, as ever; it was a ritual of twenty years or more, went to the White Fathers mass at nine o'clock. It was a damp dreich, foggy night - something like my mood -and the taxi driver lost his way and -unusual for her, my sister, Mary, became very angry and, finally, when we reached the chapel, she told me not to pay the fare.

I thought this was a bit harsh, but went along with it and we paid nothing. The journey, for what it's worth, was two miles at best, and we had been sat in the taxi for a good half hour and were late for the mass, if; later, when Mary was in hospital, she said she wished that we had paid. So, it had hung in her mind, what in truth, I had forgotten all about.

It is a small chapel and elderly priests, and, that Christmas Eve, only three of them were on the altar, where, before, on the Christmas Eve of bygone years, there had been ten or twelve or even more of them. Men who had retired from the missions in Africa. Kenya had been a favourite place, where, it would seem, they had done good work for, today, there are many black priests from Kenya

We sat in a front pew and Mary put on a show -for she was not herself, not at all -and, when the mass was ended there was a buffet of sorts and she drank some tea and spoke to lots of people. She was a chatty, friendly sort, and it was no problem to get a lift back home. But I had been watching, she had eaten nothing, not a bite, and she had been losing weight and complaining about nausea and, in short, I was very worried about her health. She had of course been to see her doctor, but it seemed to me, had been brushed off with ineffective medicines and I had urged her to see a private consultant or, failing that, to call an ambulance and present herself as an urgent case, which by now she certainly was.

It was no go. She would not hear of an ambulance or a specialist. I think she was frightened they would diagnose what she feared, for she was no fool, confirmed. And so was I, for that matter. No-one wants to know the worst until it is unavoidable.

Mary was small, barely five feet tall. She was almost 78 years old. Her birthday was the following day,25th December. She had worked part time as a parking lot attendant until June of the year when, because of her health, she had been forced to quit. I had been glad of that, her finishing work; because, I thought she had an already worked too long, but I did not like the reason for her leaving.

Up until this time there had been no pain, just a lack of appetite and a general lethargy. She was staying indoors almost all of the time, and that was most unlike her. We had arguments because of this, and her refusal to seek treatment, too, in sum, submit to tests, which, more than once had been suggested by the medical centre where she attended.

For myself, all the time, my ailing sister whom I loved, I was out of my mind with worry. But at least, and against all odds, she had made Christmas mass, and, for a short time afterwards, a week or two, appeared - for she was eating again, a light meal at least - to be herself again.

This lent me hope, that she would regain weight and a return to health and energy. It was not to be., and she was beginning to act oddly, out of character. We lived not far from one another and I was spending hours in her house. Day and night. I would visit her around twelve, one o'clock and stay until three and return at six for another few hours, but, sometimes, I was no sooner home than she would telephone me that she was frightened and I would return again and try to reassure her. The problem was that I was frightened myself regarding her health, and she was now complaining about a pain. This pain was high on her chest, just above her breast bone. When I asked when this, the pain had started, she said that it was before Christmas but it had become worse. What to do? I threatened to call an ambulance, but it was only that, a threat. She was terrified of hospital, and it ended up that she phoned in the doctor. By this time Mary had agreed to an endoscopy, which is a camera down the throat. A date had been fixed and I would go with Mary for the test. It never came to that, as she was no longer able to swallow.

She was taken by ambulance to hospital and there was no kidding myself now about what the diagnosis would be. In a blunt manner, the doctor told us she had terminal cancer and nothing could be done.

Mary died ten days later, and I am so thankful that in later life we had become so close and had spent so much time together on all the pilgrimages.

DOUBTING THOMAS

MARY

It was news to me, St Jude's shrine in Germany's Black Forest. "In a place called St Margen," my sister, Mary, told me. I had never heard of St Margen or the shrine to St Jude who, so it is said, is the patron saint of hopeless cases. I would come to know him well, St Jude: the patron of hopeless cases.

We had flown from Glasgow to Hamburg and then, by bus and train, to Freiberg, where we stayed the night. The following day, on another bus, we were in the Black Forest on our quest to find St Jude.

"When did this St Jude live?"

"In the time of Christ" Mary said. "He was one of the apostles and a kinsman of Jesus."

***

Mary has been a Catholic all her life. Not me, though; and for a time, I had wished that I was Jewish. This was back in the fifties when I was a boy and had met a girl and thought to be in love. Her name was Judith. We had met at a carnival in Glasgow Green on a summer's night and I had walked her home. She stayed not far from me, in Nicholson Street, in the Gorbals, where, at that time, there was a sizable Jewish community. We were both, aged about eleven. A long time ago, but I remember it so clearly. A rare clarity. How I felt and how she looked, all trim and neat and dark and bright and wonderful to me.

I began to hang around her street, where there were men with beards and long black coats and, all in all, a different culture. I wished it *was* my culture. Anything to be with her, my first love or crush or whatever you might call it. Not that I did anything. I was much too young and so was she, but; and it went on for months, a longing just to be with her, and we had become close enough for holding hands when - it was now October or November – one of the nights, on her street, we stood speaking for a while.

I forget our conversation, but I remember her; how she looked and what she wore and how I felt about her.

"Dirty Jew."

There were two of them, boys of about thirteen; and

the biggest one began to push at Judith who, clearly, and I could hardly blame her, those spiteful boys, was badly startled and alarmed.

"Leave her alone." I was not the bravest of boys, but how dare they speak to her that way. My beautiful girl. It was the first time I had stuck up for anyone.

"She's with me."

"She's a fucking Jew."

I hit the boy who said that. A punch on the nose. He yelped in pain and almost simultaneously his mate smashed a brick into my face, splitting my eye wide open. At the corner, in on my nose, and the boys took off and Judith screamed and I ran home.

"I thought his eye was out," my mother said, speaking to my father."

"I prayed to St Jude, but I was sure he had lost his eye."

That, then; back from hospital, with my eye stitched up and my head swathed in a bandage, was the first I had heard of a saint named Jude.

Mary has a wild fear of cats. This might well date

back to her days in the old slum- land Glasgow tenements where there were groups of cats; and some of them fierce, making humphs and spitting at you, on outside, common stairway. She was never attacked that I know of, but the fear of attack can be very, very frightening. Then again it could have been nothing, just a phobia, pure and simple. I don't know, but the cat business was very real and a real nuisance and I had to ask the proprietor of the guest house in St Margen - her name was Monika- if she owned a cat. This was not easy as she knew no English and I no German. To try and explain I began to meow. Monika with a bewildered look. No wonder. A grown man meowing like a cat.

Then a sudden smile and a knowing look, she went in back and returned with a glass of milk. Eventually, after much hilarity, it was sorted out that there was no cat on the premises, and we booked in on a half board basis. This was a lucky break, finding Monika's; as was just round the corner from the chapel.

That aside she was a good hostess and clean comfortable rooms and the best of German cuisine. A small problem, the chapel was closed and neither Monika or anyone else we spoke to knew anything about St Jude.

"I told you it was a small shrine", Mary said.

"It must be almost invisible. This is hardly a large town, yet no-one seems to have heard of it."

Mary said we would see, find out. "We're only here, after all."

We had walked around town and were now back at Monika's. Sitting in the lounge. A boozy, smoky atmosphere and two tee-total pilgrims looking for St Jude. It was, I thought - and I had my eye on Monika who was a widow in her forties and very very attractive- an unlikely place to find him. But the view was good. Monika. She wore tight blue jeans and had bright blue eyes and watching her my thoughts were far from holy. So, it goes. A pretty woman, and I had an eye for pretty women if, for some reason – that I was never able to commit – I remained a single man.

I fancied Monika, but would get nowhere. Not the first time I had fancied a woman and got nowhere. Not that I tried, not with Monika, and would doubt that she knew that I fancied her.

The following morning after breakfast we went to the chapel for ten o'clock mass. It was a sparse congregation. About thirty souls in a place that, pew upon pew, all of them empty, could easily have held a thousand. Then again it was a week day morning and, of necessity; as in chapels all over the world, attended mainly by the elderly.

But it is always nice to visit a new chapel. The altar and statues, different saints, the Stations of the Cross, are all that little bit different, one chapel to the other. I have, in various chapels, encountered saints that I had never heard of. So, a bit of exploring after mass, which had been said by a young blonde-haired priest.

Our quest for St Jude. I had expected his statue to be in the chapel, but there was no such thing. St Joseph and St Anthony, St Peter, but no St Jude. Finally, though, we encountered a man who understood what we were about and pointed us in, as it were, the right direction.

It was a lovely, blue-skyed day and we crossed over a wide flat road and down into a dirt track that had high hedges on either side. At the end of the track stood a small, sturdy, white-walled chapel and, at last, inside of it, a statue of St Jude. But a forsaken shrine if there was ever one, with nobody there but us. My sister and me, and I was hardly a believer.

There had been people there before us, though quite a few, and from unlikely places. They had left messages for other pilgrims crediting the saint with amazing cures. Some truly miraculous, out of this world happenings. People who had been cured of cancer, after; that was, the doctors had given up on them - one message, written in Spanish, was from a man who had been given three months to live. At most. He had still been alive some six years later, thanks to St Jude, his intercession.

Some might say, and I might myself if I had not read the letter, that it was a false alarm, a medical mistake.

After reading the letter I was not so sure and, should it come to the bit, I would go along with a divine intervention, no matter how crazy it might sound. This man had come from Mexico and he had already prayed to Our Lady of Guadeloupe who (I was piqued enough to read up on it later} had appeared to a peasant in Mexico City in the fifteenth century. They had later built where she had appeared and it might well have been the Lady of Guadeloupe who had directed him to the shrine of St Jude in Germany. The other letters, if equally spectacular, were without the ring of sheer truth that I had detected in the Mexican's.

The strange thing, though, we did not encounter another person at the shrine in the five days we were there, in St Margen. Then again, as my sister said, it is a little-known shrine as, for many years, St Jude was a little-known saint. He was, however, present at the Last Supper, along with the other apostles and has gained in popularity in recent times. He is often depicted carrying a club or axe. This is a symbol of his martyrdom, as it is believed that he was hacked or clubbed to death.

At the shrine, inside the chapel, I felt a peace come over me that I had never felt before. I did not mention this to Mary, as she well knew that I was not religious and might have *got* religion. It happens. Sometimes. The worst of sinners can turn into saints. So, they say, if I had yet to meet one. Yet again, in the chapel; as all my worries were swept away, I had pause for thought. St Jude. The patron saint of hopeless cases. By night-time though I had shrugged it off as my imagination.

***

Monika had a couple of young girls helping her out with the evening meal. They were all done up in their national costume. Long loose dresses and flat, clog-like shoes. It was the opposite of glamorous and something of a disappointment. You saw no shape or curve, and, certainly, it was not the dress for Monika who had a tight, plump rump much more suited to clinging jeans than this drab garb.

After our meal, a good one; nourishing food and plenty of it- a lot of Germans are overweight, and it would be easy to become fat in Germany - we went out for a coffee in a cafe which, we soon discovered, was a haunt for bikers.

Not the outlaw, hairy type. But plenty of leather and plenty of bikes, and too much drinking, pitchers of beer, for riding motorbikes. But nothing to do with me, if, one sure thing, I would have reneged on a pillion ride from one of them. Wild times.

The hefty burghers, and who was I to criticise? The chances were they had been drunk before and would be drunk again and, how such things go, would not have any accidents. It is usually the completely unexpected that will get you.

***

In the morning it was ten o' clock mass again and another visit to St Jude's. I was, in a way, beginning to be full of him. St Jude. The peace in his chapel. A sort of contentment, if I can't think why- I was far from a contented man - or, perhaps, if it might sound strange, the magic of the saint. We would linger there for a couple of hours, but I had no faith and could not pray and so it was the strangest thing the peace I felt. But there are many things I can't explain and it is better to let it go at that. We went to the shrine twice a day, in the morning and again at night. He was the only reason we were there, in that part of Germany, and it was good to see Mary's delight at the shrine of her favourite saint.

This was 2001. I was 57 years old and, given the life had led, in surprisingly good health. A few years back I had had a book published, *A hurting business*. While not a best seller it was successful enough to afford me some financial freedom. I had been writing, or trying to write since my late twenties, but with little commercial success. This had rankled me in the early days, and the fact I was a Catholic; or I was supposed to be, could not have helped me either, not in a bigoted Scotland. But I had persevered at short story writing and, eventually, my stories were published here and there and in the Saturday Extra of The Glasgow Herald. The then editor was a man named Alistair Warren who was a true gentleman and a poet. It was a blow to me when, in the early seventies, he had a row with his board and saw fit to leave the newspaper, leaving me - for the new guy did not like my writing – without a market for my stories.

My stories were hard to write and now, with Alistair gone, even harder to get published and I gave up on writing for some years. It was a mean time, those years; working manual jobs and drinking heavily; and when, finally, I began to write again it was on a flop of a novel that earned me three hundred pounds. But enough of that, and I was treating Mary to the Black Forrest on the proceeds of another book, A Hurting Business. On future pilgrimages she would pay or I would pay, until, after a while, I was none too sure who was paying. Not that it mattered, she is my sister, after all.

"What do you think of it" she asked, "St Jude's shrine?"

"I think it is peaceful."

Mary said it was more than that to her. "

"I'm glad you like it."

"I just love it." We were outside the little white-walled chapel. "It's a dream come true.

"But there's nobody here but us."

Mary exclaimed that was part of its charm. "It's like a hide-away."

I agreed. "It's next best to a secret."

***

After I stopped drinking, I could not take my mind off

women and thought to have swapped one addiction for another. I can't say that it bothered me, and I did not like an empty bed and I was full of thoughts of a troublesome past and sleep did not come easily.

This state of affairs came to an end when I met a woman in a library in March, 2001. Rosie had big brown animated eyes, and we hit it off straight away. I learned she had been married twice, but she would not give her age away. What woman does? It hardly matters, and she was the beginning of the longest, most loving relationship of my life. There is, and has always been, a lot of morbidity in my nature, where Rosie has a high, gay spirit that, when I am down, can help to lift me up again.

One of the nights she happened to ask how it would have been had we met in our twenties?

"Disastrous," I told her.

We met, Rosie and me, at the right time, stage in our lives and, I hope, I've lightened up her life a little. as she has lightened mine.

***

Glasgow is a much-changed place from the city of my youth. Early childhood. The old tenements, cobbled streets and hissing gaslights. My father worked as a quarryman and he died of a heart attack on a bus on his way to work on a Saturday in October, 1957.

This was a terrible blow, and I have often wondered if I ever really recovered from it. That quarryman. He had bright blue eyes and was strongly built and strong in his religion. Roman Catholic, what else? He was 46years old. I remember, around that time, a hit song by Connie Francis, *Who's sorry now?*

The chapel, St Bonaventures, was at the head of our street, opposite a rag store. The parish priest was a Father Gilmartin, who was bog Irish. As ignorant a man as I have encountered, and a portly, pompous one to boot. I remember his visit to our house to charge my mother a one-pound note for burying my father. I thought this mean, for she had nothing, and afterwards I hated him and everything he stood for.

This was a first for me, a fierce hatred; and the pity was that the cause of it was a Roman Catholic priest. My father had been next door to a priest himself. A wonderful, can you call it that, devotion. There was no Sunday or evening service or saint's day when he was not at the chapel. Then there were weekday nights when he would have us all kneel and say the rosary. Mary and me would make faces at each other, fed up with him and his endless prayer.

If ever a man went straight to heaven it had to be my father. But back on earth, with now no or little supervision, it was not long before I got into trouble. I must have burgled twenty, thirty shops before, one bad night - it was again October, this one year on from my father's death- I finally was caught and, together with another boy, was sent to a remand home named Larchgrove. This was a rebellious time and my mother was out of her head with worry. After a short stay in Larchgrove I was put on probation for a couple of years, but it did not make me change my ways and I soon ran away to London.

I was fourteen years old and so was my mate, the boy I ran away with. We were at school together, and it was all a laugh; if a heartless one, when we stole aboard a night-time train.

***

If I had not prayed at the shrine to St Jude in St Margen, I did light some candles. Two For my parents and one for Mary and another for my late dog, Martin, who, I'm sure – if I can't say why –I will meet up with once again. "I bet Martin is the first dog to have a candle lighted for him here, in St Jude's chapel," Mary said.

"Martin was more than just a dog to me."

"St Jude will know that."

"Do you think?"

"I'm sure of it."

***

We, Joe McGuigan and me - the boy I went to London with - had managed to rob a man on the train for something like twenty pounds, which was a lot of money then, in 1958. Off of the train and on to the platform we were caught in a rush of people, so it was easy to dodge the ticket collectors. We had been dodging ticket collectors all the way from Glasgow as, needless to say, we were travelling for free.

Once inside the station proper, we found a restaurant and ordered two slap-up breakfasts. This was a London of pin-striped suits, of bowler hats and umbrellas; a *staid* place, or so it seemed, if I was soon to discover otherwise. After our breakfast McGuigan went in to a newspaper shop and the next I knew he was arrested, for; as I later learned, stealing a bar of chocolate.

This was a dreadful *blow* for both of us. McGuigan locked up in a cell and me alone in London. What to do? Our whole adventure turned upside-down. The next I knew a man tried to pick me up, and; for he was an insistent sort, I had to fight to free myself from him.

Out from the railway station I walked in circles and walked for hours, until, about eight that night, I met with a young prostitute in King's Cross. Her name was Lily and she came from Glasgow and, how such things go; or went for me, I stayed with her for the next five days. There was nothing wrong with Lily who, I think, became fond of me and I was fond of her. My first lover. The wonder of a woman. It was at her urging, and she paid my train fare, that I returned to Glasgow.

I was no sooner off the train in Glasgow Central than I was arrested by the police. I was questioned about the man we – Joe and me - had robbed on the train on the outward journey. I said it was news to me and after a little my mother came and took me home.

By then it was early morning and icy cold and my mother was wrapped up in a shabby coat and I could see she had been crying. Walking through the gas lit streets with the tenements all in darkness. This, then, at that time, was Glasgow's Gorbals in its prime, the worst of slums in Europe.

"Why did you run away?"

"I don't know."

"I was frightened you might have been murdered."

"I'm sorry, mammy."

"You won't run away again, will you?"

"I won't run away again."

**

It is easy to knock faith, and the lucky ones are those

who have it, for it is a very special gift. Faith. The way of the cross. The Virgin Mary. She appeared, so it is said, to a young peasant girl named Bernadette Soubirous in Lourdes in France in 1858. At that time Lourdes was an impoverished, isolated village of no or little account to the outside world. Bernadette was about to change all that when, aged fourteen, she had a vision of a beautiful lady who, inside of a grotto, informed her that she was the queen of heaven, the Immaculate Conception.

The term, Immaculate Conception, had come about when the local priest, a Father Peyramale, had prompted Bernadette to ask the lady who she was. There was no way she could have come by this expression- Bernadette was next to being illiterate- other than a priest or some other religious had put the words into her mouth, but I don't think so; if I don't know why I don't think so, such a lofty information. The beautiful lady – she was dressed in a white veil and blue girdle and had yellow roses at her feet – was to appear eighteen times to Bernadette.

My sister loved Lourdes where, along with many other pilgrims, she was submerged in the healing holy water that had sprung from the ground when, on the instructions of the Lady, Bernadette had dug up the earth with her bare hands. Lourdes was our first pilgrimage after Germany, and the change was huge. St Margen had been peace and quiet, the little white-walled chapel to St Jude where there had been nobody there but us. Lourdes was the opposite, with pilgrims by the thousand; tall hotels and outside cafes and priests and nuns and religious shops and it even bragged some beggars.

We were there is November, as part of a group from a parish in Argyle in Scotland. I would think most pilgrims in Lourdes are with a group. It is the easiest, most convenient way to go there. Our group was graced with two priests and a bishop and we stayed in a hotel that was near to the Grotto.

Everywhere is Lourdes leads to the Grotto, because without the Grotto there would be no Lourdes as it is today. A thriving town to say the least, and all built on religion. When Mary asked what I thought of it I said I did not know, and neither I did. On one hand it is overpriced, the hotels and shops and cafes, but, for all of that, the piety is very real. Heartbreaking in a way! The care of the sick, and Lourdes has more than its share of the sick, the chronically ill. Wheelchairs and stretchers are commonplace and it has a hospital to help care for them. The hospital is staffed by volunteers and two of the ladies in our group; nurses both, spent all of their pilgrimage, a stay of one week, working in the hospital. I was impressed by this, who wouldn't be? The care of the sick, and the care of the sick is a big, big thing in Lourdes.

So are umbrellas. Lourdes would beat Seattle for rainfall, and it is damn cold too with an icy wind from the Pyrenees — Lourdes sits at the foot of the Pyrenees — that, in November, would have you wish for a Russian hat, a fur coat. This did not dampen the spirit of the pilgrims, who, in the evenings, in the dark, would make long candle-lit processions. The only problem as I found out it is a trouble to keep your candle lit and your hand from freezing while holding it. But a small complaint and it does not bear comparison to the wheelchair and stretcher cases that abound in Lourdes.

We were taken to Bernadette's house, which is more or less compulsory for every pilgrim who comes to Lourdes. In photos that we have of her, when she was fourteen, she looks like a delightful vagabond. There was nothing of the worldly things in the life of Bernadette. The house is in a quiet, back-street part of town and, given this, it as a walk in time; to the way things were, how they used to be, inside the house of Bernadette. A humble dwelling with wooden floors and wooden beds and pots and pans and a big wood-burning fire. The toilet facilities were outside and – you are not allowed to visit them – I would think quite primitive. The peasant girl who once lived here and has since become an icon, a shining light of the Catholic church. Bernadette was not long for this world, dying – a nun in a convent of tuberculosis – aged thirty-five. A short, eventual life that I am sure secured her place in heaven, wherever; in whatever void, that might be.

***

Home from London I was soon out of school and acquired a job as a message boy for a sheet music publisher. I hated this job but was forced to stick it because if I quit the youth employment would have stopped my benefit. What to do? I decided to take a chance and; all alone one night, I burgled a pub to obtain the funding to start up in business for myself. My business was selling coal briquettes – this was coal dust compressed into blocks that were good to back-up a fire – from a push cart I hired from a place in a lane, a sort of stable – they hired out horses too, big Clydesdales – where it was cash on the button before you got the cart. It was cash on the button for the briquettes too, and the briquette selling was damn hard work. Pushing the cart from morning till night, delivering the briquettes to house doors. I sold mine a little cheaper than the other traders and soon, for I was young and full of energy, I progressed to a horse and bigger cart and was selling sacks of coal along with the coal briquettes.

I was soon earning, easily, ten times the money I had been paid by the music publisher. A problem was that people did not burn fires in the summer, so it was very much a winter job. Late September till March or April. The trick was to save enough money to last out though the idle months, until it was winter once again.

***

Since returning from London, I had had lots of

girlfriends. The local lassies who hung around the streets at night. It was all good fun and no commitment. None at all. They came and went and, from my end at least, no hard feelings. I was a sociable, happy boy and I have often wondered what went wrong, the man I would become. One of the days around that time I was stopped by a girl in the city centre, who called me Tam, and, "It is you, isn't it?"

I stopped and smiled and all the old, as welling feeling, was with me once again.

"How are you, Judith?"

"I'm fine, but I thought you might have forgotten me."

"Then you must be daft, if you thought I might have forgotten you." It was early summer and she was dressed in a light white coat. A much bigger, fuller girl than the one I used to know, but, still, at the eyes, the way she smiled, my sweet love from long ago.

"It's great to see you, Judith."

"It's great to see you too, Tam."

We went for a coffee, and I was crazy about her all over

again.

"I missed you when we moved away," she told me.

"Not as much as I missed you."

"I was worried about your eye for ages."

"It healed."

"Thank goodness."

"I was nuts about you, did you know that?"

"I suspected you might be."

"You still look terrific."

"Thank you, Tam."

"You were only a wee girl."

"You were only a wee boy."

"I know," I said. "But I fancied you like crazy."

"You were a strange wee boy."

"How do you mean. Strange?"

"Following me."

"I was attracted to you."

"You tried to protect me."

"I remember." Looking at her, all big dark eyes and olive skin that was as smooth as alabaster.

"I hated those boys." Judith touched my eyebrow, in on my eye. "Is that the scar where the brick hit you?"

"It is."

"You were really brave." I laughed.

"I think I was more trying to impress you."

"You did."

"But it didn't get me very far, did it?"

"That was because my family moved away, out of the Gorbals."

"Where did they go?" She told me Giffnock, a place of wealth; of big houses. "My father is a dentist, did I tell you that?"

"No, you didn't!"

"Well, he is; and he began to make money and we moved out."

"What do you do, Judith?"

"I'm a student."

"Studying What?"

"Medicine." Her voice was posh, upper class; which, for some reason, made me want her even more. "I hope to become a doctor."

"That's good."

"How about you; what do you do, Tam?"

"I sell coal."

"Do you mean you are a coalman?"

"I suppose I do."

"It's heavy work, is it not – humping bags of coal."

"But only in the winter," I told her. "I've the whole of the summer off."

"Me too," Judith said, "or most of the summer. It's the one good thing about being a student, that you get lots of holidays."

"Do you have a boyfriend, Judith?"

"No, I don't. Do you have a girlfriend, Tam?"

"No." We had progressed to sort of touching hands. "I'm still nuts about you,

Judith."

"After all this time?"

"It's only six years or something."

"Only?"

"It feels like it was yesterday."

"I'm glad you think so."

"You don't?" Judith said she was almost eighteen. "I was only eleven or something when I last saw you."

"I Know."

"I'm a woman now."

"You certainly are." In event, all this; all out of the blue, we arranged to meet the following night and, in a small hotel on the Great Western Road, we ended up in bed together.

***

We had been going together, lovers in love; or so I though, for about three months when I suggested — because she was Jewish and I was Catholic and I knew there would be difficulties– that we start anew in London.

"Nobody would know us there."

"Are you suggesting that I go missing?"

"I'm suggesting that you phone home when we are in London."

"Do you mean to tell my family that I am safe?"

"That's the idea."

"It all sounds pretty desperate."

"These are desperate times – your family would never approve of me, Judith."

"Would your family approve of me?"

"You would need to become a Catholic."

"I couldn't do that."

"That's what I mean and it is why we have to leave Glasgow."

Judith agreed, if I thought a bit reluctantly – she had much more to lose than I had – but, finally, it was arranged that we would make a run for it.

***

In the Central Station, waiting for Judith. I was all bagged-up, ready to go. The night train down to London. We would made out somehow, someway. I was sure of that, but; and she was already late, as the time drew near for the train to go – it departed from Platform 2 – I was not so sure about my lover. I had bought our tickets, one way. An escape from a hostile, un-understanding city. So, I had thought. But minutes to go and there was still no Judith. I watched the last passengers, some of them running to board the train, and there was no hope, not now. I gathered my baggage and began to walk out of the station when I was accosted by a dark-haired man.

"Are you Tam?" I said I was.

"I'm Judith's father."

"How do you do?" Those were my exact words.

"All the better," he told me, "That Judith has stood you up."

I was a tall, thin, youth; and he was short and portly. An aggressive approach. It was what I thought, anyhow. On the night, inside the Central Station. A dentist. I would have liked to have slackened a few of his teeth. "Did Judith ask you to speak to me?"

"She did! That's the reason I'm here. She told me all about your wicked plot." I was too down, broken hearted; as betrayed by Judith, to argue with him.

"You are a heartless man," he told me, "All the worry you would have caused." I said nothing.

"She gave me this to give to you," the father said, and he handed me a pink envelope. "It's all in there, I think," he said, "why she did not meet you."

I walked away without a word and on the street outside the station tore up the envelope and I hated Judith more that night than I had ever loved her.

***

Jerusalem. It has a magic, majestic ring. All through the bible it is heavily featured. Jesus Christ. The garden of Gethsemane. Golgotha. The Last Supper. On the third day, He rose again. Good Friday to Easter Sunday when Catholic altars are bright with flowers. A Christian jubilation! Jesus had died and was buried in a sepulchre, but on the third day, on Easter Sunday, He rose again. It is the Apostles' creed and in every chapel in the world there are the Station of the Cross. Jesus falls for the first time. The Stations are still there today, in Jerusalem; the highlight, could you call it that, of a tortuous, earthly end.

In primary school in the Glasgow of the fifties you had the Christ story rammed down your throat. The priest was a frequent visitor. You were told of the three wise men and how they had followed a bright star and found the baby Jesus and outfoxed Herod who, for reasons that were not made clear, had murder on his mind. It was too much for me and I shut down, and I was still shut down; religious wise, when, together with a group of pilgrims, Mary and me flew from Glasgow to Tel Aviv to view the land where it had all begun, the Christian faith and, out of it, the childhood stories of long ago.

Our first stop was Nazareth. This after a six-hour flight and two hours to clear customs at Ben Gurion airport. So, we were all tired, worn out, on the bus to Nazareth, where we would stay for only one night, but long enough for a visit to Mary's Well. Jesus had been raised in this place so it stands to reason that He had drunk the water from the well. But a down at the heel, disagreeable place; disgruntled Arabs, and I was glad to see the back of it when, the following day, we moved on to Bethlehem were we would reside for the remaining six days of our pilgrimage.

It was another disappointment, Bethlehem. An appalling poverty, and, really, The Holy Land was turning out to be far from holy in my eyes. Our hotel was a Spartan place that served rotten food, but at least you could smoke in it. A coffee and a cigarette. Small things sometimes mean a lot. They meant a lot to the Arabs outside who, every morning, when we departed the hotel to go on our bus, would try and sell us something. Bangles and beads, worthless things, and how they survived I do not know.

Now and then our bus was stopped at checkpoints by armed Israeli soldiers. Not a peaceful place, the Holy Land; with, what it is and no mistake, a mutual hatred between Jew and Arab. That aside, we would continue on to whatever place we had to see that day, and our first stop on our first day was Galilee where, at the feast in Cana, Jesus had worked His first miracle, changing water into wine. It was a fitting setting, on the grass above the sea of Galilee, for our opening mass of our pilgrimage. The altar was a small, white-clothed table that folded up and was easy to carry in our journey though the Holy Land. I will never forget that mass; in the sun, it was July, and the priests – there were two of them – in clothes of brilliant white and the glittering gold of their chalices. A solemn, pious happening where it had all begun, the dawn of Christianity.

Holy Communion. The body (a sliver of bread) and blood (a sip of wine) of Christ. But not for me. You must, to partake of Holy Communion, be free of sin and a good confession in order, and I had not been to confession since I was twelve years old. Still, it would be true to say that for the very first time; in the sun on the grass in the field above the sea of Galilee, I felt a little envious of the true believers.

Another troubling, worrying thing I had found myself seriously attracted to a young woman in our group of pilgrims. She was there with her husband to pray to have a baby. I put the blame on him, naturally. But it was not right, not on pilgrimage, shades of Monika – but much, much stronger – to have such feelings, and I could hardly take my eyes off her.

We spoke not a word the whole pilgrimage, but such an

attraction; and I would fantasise about her for all I knew that it was hopeless. That said, she enchanted me as, I'm sure, Salome had enchanted Herod and won the head of John the Baptist.

My attraction, strong as it was, could hardly be compared to that and, really, it was no big deal, just a normal man and woman thing, if, in this instance, I would doubt the woman knew. So, it goes! Secret lusts. And some not so secret. They have happened though the ages, and; really, for they are as natural as breathing, nothing to be put out about.

A couple of days later we would visit the Jordan – it is much more a dirty stream than a flowing river - where John had preached and baptized sinners and, somehow, incurred the wrath of Salome's mother, a woman named Herodias, who put her daughter up to it, her dance and the head of John the Baptist. Bethlehem. The Church of the Nativity, where, deep in a bunker underground, was the stable in the manger, the birthplace of Christ; if it is hard to imagine, when in this place; for it is all dark and cavernous, that it once was open countryside with rolling fields and sheep outside.

On the exact spot where He was born there is a gold star on white marble that must have been kissed a million time and, all those pressing lips, would appear to be now worn hollow. One short kiss is all you get before you are hurried on. Up again, on steel spiral steps, into the blazing sun where we had a group photo taken in the forecourt of the church.

On the bus I asked Mary what she had thought of it, the star; where, as aeons past, on a different level, the manger had once been. She said she had thought it spooky.

"So did I."

"It's like a strange nether world down there."

"That's a good description."

"It's the best that I can manage."

"I think it's as good as anyone could manage."

Back again in our hotel for our miserable evening meal. It was mostly rice and vegetables with a bit of meat or chicken, and most of the pilgrims were suffering upset stomachs of varying severity. I escaped that fate and so did Mary, but only by sheer luck.

"It's as bad as Delhi belly," an old army man of a pilgrim told me. "My wife has had a doctor in and she is still in bed."

"She is not the only one from what I've heard."

"Far from it," he said. "That doctor guy must be coining in a fortune." In the morning, bright and early; before the heat of the sun —and the summer sun in Israel strikes down like an anvil — we, what fit pilgrims still remained, were again on the bus, going to Jerusalem.

David's Royal city. The wailing wall. This is the remains of the first temple that was built by David's father, King Solomon. This, in time, is much closer to Moses than to Christ. Jerusalem has a rare smell — I wonder did it has it then, in the time of David and of Christ? - something akin to cinnamon and not at all unpleasant. But much unpleasantness has happened here, in this city. The Way of the Cross. It is still there and is easy to find for it is thronged with pilgrims. A place of narrow cobbled streets that; in truth, founded a religion, but what a way to start it. Under a cross and staggering, falling down. Christ fell three times according to the scriptures. Lashed and mocked and jeering crowds. Good Friday. I can see nothing good about such a day, what happened in Jerusalem all those years ago. But without Good Friday there would be no Catholic Church or Christian faith, and who am I to argue? The House of the Last Supper. Whether it was or not I don't know. But we found ourselves in a hall with high ceilings and white-washed walls where Jesus – knowing what was to become of him, in his human form – prophesied he would be betrayed and that Peter would deny him three times before the cock crowed thrice.

An interesting, busy day; and the following one we were to return to Jerusalem, this time unaccompanied. Until then, as a group; we had been shepherded by a Palestinian named Hassam, who was good at his job and a likable man, if; now and then when he slipped up, it was clear he was anti-Jewish. On our free day Mary and I decided to visit the Yam Vaster Holocaust Museum.

Once again it was an early start, but not too early for the beggars, the trinket sellers – they were all men, not a woman in sight – to try to extract some shekels. Most of the pilgrims gave them a swerve, but most of the pilgrims did not know true poverty. We did, my sister and me, and I made a point to have some shekels to give to them.

Many a Palestinian, Hassam for one; and Gaza must be full of them, would cheer a new coming of Adolf Hitler. Der Fuhrer. Yet, ironically; in a huge way, this foe of the Jews, he began the State of Israel. As that, after him, the Jewish people had had enough and, a new hard breed – a hardness forced upon them – determined, come what may, to have a Jewish homeland. This of course was bad news for the Arabs, but they had no say, choice in the matter – not with determined settlers who had the backing of America, and world opinion on their side after the horror of the Hitler years. Six million dead, gassed or starved, and I have read Mein Kampf where Hitler makes no secret of his hatred of the Jews. A lot of Germans must have read it too, yet he was voted into power It is a warning that, I am sure, has not been forgotten by the Jewish people, especially when; as has often happened in the past, their Arab neighbours have risen up to destroy the State of Israel. Inside the Holocaust Museum – it is on a hill and there is a wonderful view of the Dome of the Rock from it – Hitler is on video, ranting against I know not what, but I would imagine the Jewish people. This is the Fuhrer at his best, or worst; I think in 1939, and he is easily the most frightening man I have ever seen. In another video, before the Hitler one – and it is all about before and after Hitler – we see Jewish children at play in a street in Warsaw. Or in Prague. It hardly matters, for it could be in New York or Rome or even Glasgow. Especially Glasgow. Judith and her pals in the tenements of the Gorbals.

They had been no different from the children in the video. A swarthy, dark-eyed happy lot, skipping rope – the girls, that is – and playing in, in all; a street like the streets I had used to know. This, for me; fond memories of Judith, was – the fate of those children when the German armies had conquered Europe - a real heartbreaker. Mary remarked, of the video,

"It's just like the Gorbals used to be." I concurred.

"I remember streets like that."

Mary knew nothing about Judith; or how, because of her, I felt a close affinity to the children in the video. We wandered here and there, in different parts of the museum. The German war with Russia in 1941 that, at last, caused Hitler pause, that his armies were not invincible. But for me, easily, the highlight was the ghetto children, happy little ragamuffins; much like me and Judith were, had been.

I have omitted a lot, our pilgrimage in the Holy Land, for it was a whirlwind trip with too much to see and too little time to take it in, as all of the bible in one week. Back home in Glasgow I told Mary all about Judith and how the children in the video had brought the whole thing back. "It was almost just like yesterday."

***

Looking back, if at the time I hated him, I can't blame Judith's father for as chasing me away. Had I been him I would have done the same, and; anyhow, when it came down to it, it had been Judith's choice to stay at home rather than go to London. It would be silly to say, at the age I was, that a woman drove me to drink, but; and I was dreadfully unhappy about losing her, she showed me the road, and that's a fact.

A few pints of beer and I could forget her, and that was good. For at that time, I was using booze rather than booze using me. At this time, the early sixties; Glasgow had begun to change. A slum clearance. The Gorbals was one of the first to go. The tumble of a hundred years, or even more. To cope with this change, and it was massive, large new housing schemes were built to re-house all the people. Not that all of them wanted re-housed. Far from it. There were people, I knew a few, who did not want to leave the Gorbals, where; for some, they had seen out two world wars and were contented in the tenements. But as it was had to go and, this demolition - and it was remarkably quick, about a year or eighteen months – meant there were no houses left to sell my coal and briquettes too and, in short, I was made redundant.

But not for long. I was a worker then if nothing else and I became a navvy. It is an almost obsolete job today, a navvy. You have mechanical diggers that have all but done away with the old pick and shovel men. But back in the sixties there were still lots of them, mostly Irish. My first job was digging ditches in a place named Linwood where they were building houses for key staff in a huge new car plant.

This was winter, late November and freezing cold. Your hands would hack, crack open with the cold. Our job was to dig gullies for water pipes, and some of them deep, like six foot down. We would begin at eight and, most nights – under lights – would continue on until about eight at night. Twelve hours. The pay was good, but beastly work and it would be safe to say that all of the navvies drank. Whisky and beer and, after work, they would be in some pub drinking every night.

There was to be no drinking on the next job I navvied at. This was in the far north of Scotland where they were building a hydro-electric scheme. Other than one guy from Newcastle – a thin, wiry, bald-headed man – all of my mates were Irish. We lived in huts and some of them would form a group and say the rosary each night. I looked on in wonderment. The Irishers called Scotland the dark country with the black heart and, stuck where I was, could only agree with that. We slept in bunk beds and there was no or little hygiene. This dig for money, and it was all about money – as a new gold-rush in the Scottish Highlands – where there was no booze and it was easy to save, for you had nothing; or only tobacco, to spend your money on.

A funny thing, all of the guys wore long johns and once a week we would put them all in a big tin tub to boil up and it was usually a fight or two when they came out, for they were all mixed-up and guys trying to claim a better pair than they had put in. That in the beginning, for as the job progressed, we were instructed to tag our belongings to ensure each man got back what he had put in. I worked at this job from early January until May or June, when, with a pocket full of money, I returned to Glasgow.

***

My first new girlfriend was named Katie, and she was on the pill, and this made for a rampant sex life. We were together for a couple of months before it fizzled out. I can't remember my next lover. Girls came and went and with them went my money, and soon I was back to navvying. It was not too hard this time around, and I was used to my fellow navvy men. A rough tough bunch, but I suppose by then I was tough myself. The thing that most astonished me about my mates, men who cursed and drank and worked as beasts – they really did, out in all weathers with their picks and shovels – was, for the sum of them, their devotion to the Catholic faith. We worked Sundays, and you could be sure that a good half of them had been to an early mass before they came to work. The navvying game was transient, and you sometimes worked twenty or thirty or even forty miles away. To get to the location you had a pick-up on the back of an open lorry that usually left from Glasgow Cross. It was nothing unusual at that time to see lorries full of navvy men on the backs of open lorries.

But there were other times when you could not get work, not if you were Scottish. Navvy gangers were always Irish and looked out for their fellow Irishmen. Indeed, at times, when work was slack, it was impossible to gain employment if you did not come from Ireland. A sad state of affairs, and when I saw a newspaper advertisement for jobs in the railway I put in an application and soon began work as a trainee shunter in the old St Enoch station in Glasgow.

For St Jude's feast day, October 28, we, Mary and me, arranged a short pilgrimage in Faversham in Kent – it is the only place in Britain where there is an official shrine dedicated to the saint. Our accommodation was to be in a pub, the Swan and Harlequin, and we began our journey on the 26th with an early morning train to London. Once there we had to cross the city from Euston to Victoria to board a bus to Faversham. A problem was, when we arrived in Faversham it was early evening and already dark, and we stayed on the bus a stop too long.

It was a long walk back, but we were two healthy pilgrims. In a warm, almost balmy night more like June or July than October. The Pen and Harlequin, when we found it, had no front lighting and was near to a brewery in a dingy-looking part of town. Mary looked at me, I looked at her. This dreary, shabby-looking place. Inside, though; it was very different, a crowded bar and a smiling host who said his name was David and showed us to our rooms. They were nothing great but not too bad for the cheap price we were paying.

A couple of minutes' walk from the pub showed a different side to Faversham. A sedate, upmarket town. There was a number of restaurants and, at that time, 2006, you could smoke indoors in England, and after my meal I enjoyed a cigarette. I still do, but, changing times; smoking bans up everywhere, it is not indoors in public any more. We sat near the window and outside, on the street, the people were lightly, gaily dressed. "I didn't think for weather like this," Mary said.

"Neither did I!"

"I hope it that it keeps up."

"It's almost like summer."

"It's better than most of the summer's we get in Glasgow." Out from the restaurant we went back to the Pen and Harlequin where David said I had a phone message and that I should call the number back.

"Guess what?" Rosie said when I got through to her.

"You've won the lottery?"

"Don't be daft."

"Then what is it?"

"The Americans have put in an offer for your book." My book I Have Heard you Calling in The Night had been published the month before, in September.

"Who told you this?" I asked Rosie.

"Ian Jack, at Granta! He thought you might be staying with me."

"Did he say how much the Americans are offering?"

"No, but he did say that it was a good offer."

***

In the morning the sun was shining, and it would continue to shine until we left Faversham. Over breakfast, I told Mary about Rosie's phone call.

"That's great," she said. "I'm really pleased for you." Later that day, I telephoned Ian Jack and the offer from a New York publisher was for fifty thousand dollars.

***

It was a short walk from the Pen and Harlequin to the chapel, the shrine to St Jude, where we attended ten o'clock mass. I was surprised to see lots of small, dark-skinned people in the congregation. I was to learn they were Sri Lankan and had come down from London on a sort of mini pilgrimage. St Jude is, if I don't know why, much revered in Sri Lanka. The shrine itself, in Faversham, is under the chapel and grilled off from the public. A lonely St Jude. In biblical clothes and sandaled feet and a big white beard and holding, in his right hand, his little axe or hatchet. As it was, I felt a giant, as a Gulliver in Lilliput;

amongst all the small Sri Lankans who had gathered at his shrine.

"St Jude was never in India, in Sri Lanka," I said to Mary, "was he?"

"Not unless he had wings."

"They would appear to have a great devotion to him."

"Many people have a great devotion to St Jude."

"But you wouldn't think in Sri Lanka."

"He is known as the miracle worker," Mary said. "Word gets around, you must know that."

"To Sri Lanka?"

"It must have done."

"That's amazing."

"So is St Jude."

***

Out from the shrine and away from the chapel we had a coffee at an outside cafe, and; weather-wise, once again it was hard to credit that this was late October.

"You must be pleased that the Americans want your book," Mary said.

"I'm more pleased about the fifty thousand dollars."

"It might do well in America."

"It might. Who knows? But I think it's a bit parochial." This turned out to be all too true, and my book was a failure in America – not that it was any big deal in Britain, either.

***

We went to two masses on the 28th, one in the morning and another at night. Once again, on both occasions; the chapel was as taken over by the people of Sri Lanka. They spoke a sing-song English and we learned from them it was better to take the train to London. It was a much shorter journey. About one hour. The bus was a long and winding way and the best part of three hours. It was cheaper of course, but, at times, you have to choose the easy way, so we decided to go home by the train.

The morning mass was simple, low key; and only one

priest, but the evening one had five priests and a bishop. There are times when there is a lot of theatre in the Catholic church, and this was one of them. The altar as become a stage, all lighted up and full of glitter. Burning candles and the bishop, who was overweight; indeed, he was, and all done up like a Christmas tree. His high office. He more than did it justice, as; for all the world, on the altar, seated in a high red chair and wearing a tall, like a foot high hat, as out of another, more flamboyant time.

It was what I thought, and Mary too. "All he needs is a wig," she said, "and he could be in the sixteenth century. I agreed. What pomp and splendour. It was, somehow, as out of place for a saint like Jude who, I liked to think, was a humble man.

In my time as a navvy, I had joined my mates for the occasional pint at finishing time, but that was all and I was never the worse of drink. The railway years were to change all that. I was twenty years old and the job was shifts and weekend work and there were plenty of pubs outside St Enoch's, and it was the same in the Central when I was shifted there, as a fully trained shunter. Not that I was drinking very heavily, not then.

There was more on my mind than alcohol. I was not bad looking and I was attracted to girls and they were attracted to me. A magical time, looking back. The money earned was surprisingly good, with a shift allowance and double time for Saturday and Sunday. I was earning as much, almost, as I had when a navvy in the Highlands, and for a lot less work. Shunting trains. It could be a dangerous job and you had to know what you were doing. Especially when, as at that time; you had the old steam engines and drunkenness was epidemic. I do not exaggerate. Not a bit. I once saw a shunter walk off a platform and smash his head on the steel track. It was a frightening sight; and I had liked the guy, and it would not have happened had he been sober. The drivers too were often drunk, and it was as well they had a fireman to help them out. How this state of affairs had come to be I do not know and never will. But it went on and on and the wonder is that the railway functioned. It is all changed now, so I have heard, but at that time the pubs outside the Central Station were full of railway workers. On duty, or supposed to be. It was the easiest thing to slip out of the station for a drink. A pint of beer that would go to two and often more and I chose to forget, I must have done, the shunter who had walked off of the platform and smashed his head on the track below, spilling out; a goodly spew, what brains he had once possessed.

***

After some months in the Central I put in for promotion to a head shunter and was transferred to a yard in Springburn. This was the worst move I could have made as, as it soon transpired, I was working with a bunch of drunks and the Springburn area was a tough, hard place, not, in a way, unlike how the Gorbals had used to be.

***

The shunting yard – it served Queen Street station in the city centre – was down a short, lane-like street that had two pubs where I often stood and drank in. With any sense I would have shunned them both, for, in either one, for the slightest slight, real or imagined, you could be easily be maimed or murdered. My job was three shifts, morning; late, and through the night. It was a seven-day week because you worked weekends and rest days, I sometimes thought that I was never out of railway gear or away from that shunting yard.

It was a busy place, for there was goods trains too and shunting wagons speeding in all directions. How no-one was killed I just don't know. There were a lot of near things, accidents; and I remember one man lost a hand when he was drunk and it was mashed between two buffers.

This did not bother me, it couldn't have, for; in no time at all, I was drinking as heavily as the next and was drunk on most weekends. Alcohol is insidious, a creeping thing; and for the want of it I began to burgle local pubs when I was working night shift. I had plenty of practice and was good at it, the burgling. I had a good nerve too,

I must have had, and I would share out the bottles with my mates. What madness! They would drink the stuff and praise me for being a game guy, but none of them offered to help me break into the pubs. But enough is enough, this chapter in my life; and sufficient to say that I had a drinking problem when I was twenty-one or, at the outside, twenty-two years old.

***

Mary suggested we went to Rome where, somewhere within the Vatican, St Jude is buried.

"But I'm not sure where!"

"In a wall," I suggested.

"I read somewhere that a lot of saints are buried in the walls." Mary said she had no idea.

"But he is definitely buried someplace there."

"I hope they have an altar to him."

"So do I."

"I mean, St Jude is special, isn't he."

"To me he is," Mary said.

"To us," I corrected.

"Do you want to go and see, to find out?"

"Sure," I said, "anything for St Jude."

The women of Rome. There are some beauties. A

legion of them. On every street, round every corner. The older I become, the more I appreciate a good-looking young woman. Perhaps, because I can no longer get one, not easily; if at all, and, usually, what is hard to get is what you want.

We stayed in a pension that, if sparse, was clean and not far from the train station. This was just as well because, along with St Jude who was somewhere in the Vatican, Mary wanted to visit Assisi; the home of St Francis, and a war grave at Anzio where our uncle, a man named Dan, was buried. We would be the first family members to visit Dan's grave in all the time he had been there, since 1944.

We had arrived in Rome on October 27th and of course, for St Jude, we were in the Vatican on the 28th. The first thing to catch my eye inside the Vatican was a horizontal marble cast of a departed pope. Who he was I do not know, but I would warrant to say he had the biggest nosed pope, ever. This lent an aura of authority, as, even in death, he featured hugely – there are no two ways about that one, such a nose – in the history of the Papal state. A city within a city in the centre of Rome. The power of the Catholic church. It will brook no law except its own. This, as a sense of power, Godly rule; is no-where more apparent than in Rome, and, especially; for me at least, in the regal cast of the big-nosed pope.

Not so for Mary. She appeared to barely notice him. Her search for St Jude. It was far from easy in this vast place of pillars and paintings and high, high ceilings. It lent the impression that; and for all the people milling there, looking at the treasures, one good shout would echo madly. Before the shouter was hustled to jail, that was. The place was full of uniformed attendants, who; to my surprise when Mary asked, had never heard of St Jude. There is nothing warm about the Vatican. It is too hard, austere; and, to my mind, as welcome as a graveyard. Mary, though; is nothing if not determined, and after a great deal of enquiry was finally shown to the altar of St Jude. I could barely credit it. St Jude. There was a mention to him, nothing more – his relics were indeed buried in the wall, so I was given to understand – at the bottom right-hand corner of a massive painting of St Joseph. I thought this pretty pathetic and said as much to Mary.

Mary said it did not matter and that St Joseph, who's altar it was, was much the better known. "But you would have thought some flowers at least to celebrate St Jude's feast day.

"People would think they were for St Joseph."

"But St Jude would know they were for him."

"The attendants wouldn't." Mary said that they might know now.

"That's something." I paused for a moment.

"You don't think we are the first people to come here looking for St Jude, do you?"

The painting of St Joseph showed an old man with a big white beard and I wondered how, at his age, he had led Mary and the child Jesus out of Israel into Egypt with only a donkey helping him.

I was to learn later, from a priest, that rather than old St Joseph had been young, in his teens or twenties, when he had made this journey.

After Mary completed her prayers and we departed the Vatican and outside it was bright sunshine and a gorgeous day in Rome. My book, I Have heard you Calling in the

Night, had been published in Italian, and; a small brag, it was a best seller in Italy and, naturally, I wanted to see it in the bookshops. And there it was, in the first bookshop we visited; a huge pile of copies and a new cover and a new title *Tio presento Martin*. Mary thought it a better cover than the English and American ones and I had to agree. A photo of a young, wistful looking pup that was supposed to be Martin, and it might well have been the cover that had sold the book. I had, and still have no idea of the Italian reviews, but one sure thing it sold an awful lot of copies.

"You must be proud to see your book for sale in a shop in Rome."

"Not proud, but pleased."

"I'm pleased for you."

"I'd trade the book to have Martin back."

"And the years."

"Them too. The strange thing is I thought I was old when I first had Martin, and I was only thirty-nine."

"It's all comparative."

"I wish it was, but I don't think so — not the way I feel

sometimes."

"I was trying to cheer you up."

"I know."

"Well, you are an author."

"Not as good an author as I wanted to be."

"I think you've done not bad."

"I could have done a whole lot better."

"We all think that when we reach a certain age." I agreed.

"The sad thing is that there is nothing we can do about it."

"Not a thing," Mary said. "You've just got to try and live with it."

***

The following day we went by train to Assisi. St Francis. I can remember reading about him at school. He gave bread to the birds and the cloak off of his back to a poor man and could communicate with wild animals. A certain bear had terrorised a village until St Francis had some words with it. His friend, St Clare, was holy too, and she founded the Carmelites, an order of nuns that is still going today. St Francis had, initially, desired to become a hermit but, by dint of his good example, other like-minded men had sought him out, including a young St Anthony. St Anthony had to be young when he visited St Francis, for he died aged thirty-three. St Francis himself was not much older, still in his thirties when he died in Assisi.

His tomb is in an underground crypt which he shares with five of his fellow monks. It is a modest affair, befitting the man, unlike the basilica above it. A somewhat gothic, garish building more in fitting for an Arab emir than the remains of the Catholic saint who founded the Franciscans. It is a clergy sworn to poverty and, as a symbol of it, the pious men of the order wear harsh brown cassocks and go bare-foot in sandals. I can remember the Franciscan chapel in Cumberland Street in the fifties, when the weather was fierce, sub-zero; snow and ice, but it did not deter the Franciscan priests and brothers you often saw outside, on the street, in their cassocks and open sandals. The glorification that is Assisi must, I think, be an affront to them and to St Francis who, in his lifetime, shunned away from all that glittered.

***

The next stop on our Italian visit was to Anzio and the war grave of our uncle Dan. Both Assisi and Anzio are about a couple of hours by train from Rome. I had enjoyed the trip to Assisi, but I was in something of a low mood, to begin with at least, on the train to Anzio. An altercation on the station concourse in Rome. Mary had thought we would miss the train, and I told her we could get another one. "It's nothing to do with you," she told me. I thought different. A beggar had a dog on a long rope lead and I had seen him kicking it. The dog had yelped in pain, and the beggar, who was a tall, thin, gipsy-looking man in a long threadbare coat, kicked it again. This in a crowded station, and I truly think the dog could have been kicked to death and still nobody would have paused to help it.

"Please don't." Mary gripped my arm.

"There's nothing you can do about it."

No, maybe not; but on the moment I was filled with rage. The bullying, dog-kicking tramp. I was about to seize him by the throat when he dropped to his knees and begged for mercy. I have met some cowards in my time, but this guy took the biscuit. He had been so brave kicking at a helpless dog that, by way of my intervention, now appeared to belong to me. I was holding its lead – a length of rope –and Mary was beside me then and we looked one to the other and down at the dog, which looked like an Alsatian cross and was skinny to not believe. All this on an instant and when Mary asked what I proposed to do with the dog I told her I did not know.

"You can't take it home with you."

"I know I can't take it home with me, but I want to try to help it."

"I don't see how you can."

"Neither do I." The brutal beggar had regained his feet and skulked away, lost in the crowded station. And it was as well that he had for had he still there I might well have set about him. As it was, I was, as so often happens – or has happened to me in my life – I was spared my dilemma by the appearance of a tall, well-dressed woman who said it was barbarous, what had happened to the dog. Mary asked this woman if there was someplace we might take the dog?

"I will take it." She would.

"I will find it a good home."

***

It is a long time since 1944 to the near-present and the Anzio war graves have few visitors. Dan's immediate family, when he died, and for years after, had been much too poor to even think to visit to his resting place, so; in all the years since he had fallen, we would be the first of his kin above his grave.

The station is a fair distance from the cemetery, and it is a poor bus service in that part of Italy. I think a bus every two or three hours. It was too long to wait if we wanted to see the grave in day light. But there was a tourist bus outside the station that I had been told – a whisper from a railway worker – was passing by the British war graves. However, when we tried to board this bus, we were refused passage, so I stood directly in front of it until the courier changed his mind, to a roar of approval from the passengers. So far so good, until; that was, we were put off at the wrong graveyard. I think the American cemetery. Still, it was not too far from the British one. Grave after grave and all young men. An average age of about twenty-one. The day was bright and the grass was green and the crosses above the graves were white and set in perfect alignment. A peaceful, well-tended place; and may they rest in peace, those soldiers. When we found Dan's grave Mary dug a small hole beside the tombstone and buried a set of rosary beads.

Out from the graveyard and on to the road - it was flat and straight and without, so far as I could see, a bus stop - we hitched a lift back to the station and, soon after that, we were returned to Rome, where; if a little too late, Mary had discovered a chapel near to the Trevi Fountain that, the day before, had had a special mass in honour of St Jude. "I wish we'd known before," she said.

I did, too. St Jude. It was strange, but it had become a habit that I would sometimes say a prayer to him. My sister had prayed to him for me and against the odds I had come through and it was only fair, as I saw it, that I returned the favour. But more, I felt the better for a prayer to him, who, as I had discovered, could sooth my troubled heart.

"We will know next time," I said to Mary,

"When we come back again to Rome."

***

I was sacked from the railway aged twenty-three. I had seen it coming but was as powerless to change my ways, to stop the drinking. I thought it manly, and masculinity – my own – has always been a big, big thing to me. I was a coward to be a coward, if that makes sense. The rough and tumble of the Gorbals. The shunting yard was no place for a weakling either. But what the fuck was I about? There was nothing to prove, not on that score anyhow. I could hold my own in the toughest company. My winter in the Highlands with the navvies, a much tougher lot than the railwaymen, had more than proven that. But some nag in my head that I had to be bolder, braver. It sounds crazy, like I was all screwed up; and I must have been, for that was the way it was. Working for the railway. I used to rob the dining cars and drink all the booze in them. My mates of course would help me with it, without, that was, taking a risk themselves. They were older, wiser men than me and that they kept their jobs while I lost my mine more than serves to prove it.

Far better had I never seen that shunting yard where, in sum; in all truth, I became a drunkard. It might have happened later, or never have happened at all. St Jude might know, but I don't. What I do know is that it would have taken longer. A few years rather than the two I spent in Springburn. It was to come to a sudden end. A train went off the rails when I was drunk, and I was sacked the following day.

I was lucky to leave that way, with nothing criminal; for the railway cops had their eyes on me and I was not stupid and knew they had their eyes on me. The looted booze from the dining cars. They had almost caught me once or twice, and I should have stopped; that it was becoming much too risky, but I could not stop from being reckless. So, the de-railed train might have been a good thing. For me. A little longer, and the chances were I would have left the job in handcuffs.

My next job was a swimming pool attendant. It was a step down money-wise from the railway. But a much easier job and no nightshift and a bit of romance with an attractive young school teacher. Her name was Betty and – I had been an avid reader since I was sixteen -we soon discovered a shared interest in literature.

At that time, I was into short stories. Jack London. Guy de Maupassant. O Henry. A whole pile of writers. Hemingway and Faulkner, Sean O'Faolain. They all had different styles but they were all good and I marvelled at the word play. A more concise work than the writing of a novel. So, I thought. The best of novels have loose writing, but there is nothing loose about a good short story. Both that and the brevity appealed to me and – for a novel was too long, time consuming – I began to try and write short stories.

Betty taught English and was appalled by my spelling and lack of grammar but was kind enough to encourage me in my try to be become a writer. To this end I had bought a typewriter, a huge pre-war machine, and had learned to type and Betty would read my stories. In her opinion they were not too bad, but that I had to learn grammar.

"I've got a rough idea."

"A rough idea is not enough."

"You could teach me."

Betty tried, I'll say that for her; but her prose, all proper English was not for me, and, at the end of the day, neither was she. A few angry words and it was all over. The easiest way to get rid of a writer, or a would-be writer is to criticise their work. But it would not have lasted anyhow, and it was best for both of us a clean, sharp break.

Alone again I began to drink more heavily. At that time, at the age I was, a woman could sometimes put the hems on me. But with Betty gone there was no woman, and I was drinking at work, in the swimming pool, where my immediate boss was an aggressive, former boxer.

His nickname was Beef because he was fat. Grossly so. Beef was far from tall but weighed in at a good two hundred pounds. At least, and that is conservative. I had rubbed along with this guy for the best part of six months. There was neither like nor dislike. He knew I drank, but I had contained my drinking until my break-up with Betty. Beef did not like this change, and neither would I had the positions been reversed. As it was, we had some words and it came to blows and, an ungainly tangle – him so fat and me so drunk – we ended up in the swimming pool. It is funny now, thinking back; a half-drowned Beef, who, what made the whole thing funnier, could not swim and was lucky to be rescued. Still, he retained his job while I lost mine and, that very night, full of drink, I was on a train to London.

***

A short time before this new adventure my mother had moved out of the Gorbals – the house we had was now empty sky – to a new place in a tenement in a scheme named Toryglen. The house was a ground flat and, along with inside facilities – a bathroom and a shower – we had a small front garden and, really, the change was almighty from the crumbling, rat-infested Gorbals.

I had helped with the decorating and we had bought new furniture and, all in all, things were looking up for us and, in the morning in Euston Station, I wished that I had stayed at home. I had no- place to go and knew no-one and, hungover in the morning, thought to be mad for being there when I could, and with a lot less effort, have found another job in Glasgow.

As it was, my wayward ways, I found a cafe and ate a greasy English breakfast. I remember that while sitting there I saw an off-sales opening across the street and after a first few drinks – in the open, out of the bottle – I felt much better. It is the way with booze, the trick of the trap, that when you come round from a drunken night a few more drinks will buck you up. They did for me that morning. In London. Without the drink, the chances were I would have been on the next train home.

I had some money, but nothing else. No change of shirt or underwear. This, all of it; my fight with Beef and now in London, was, for I had not planned on either one, the work of booze, pure and simple. The sad thing was that I could not see it, what was staring me in the face. I put it down for a one-off thing that, in time; after similar strange awakenings, I would begin to accept as part of the price of the drinking game.

Later that morning I found a low-rent room and the very next morning I was working on a building site. I was young and strong and London, this was the summer of 1967, was a swinging city. Make love not war was a popular slogan and I was all for that. Scott McKenzie's, if you are going to San Francisco was a huge hit and, during that summer of love, as it came to be known, young people did wear flowers in their hair.

I was caught up in it, this; what it was, a gentle revolution, all the barriers as crashing down and I would think the beginning of gay culture. There were lots of boys who looked like girls, and acted like them too. Nobody cared. Do your thing. I could not have agreed more. The London of 1967. I was working hard on the building sites but I was full of sap and, seemingly, it was how I felt, fit enough for anything. Could I choose an age to remain through life it would be twenty-three. It is all downhill, a creeping decline, afterwards. But you do not know it at the time and think to stay that way, aged twenty-three, forever.

I had acquired a girlfriend who was upper class and had lots of money. She was older than me, in her forties; what, to begin with at least, I had thought as ancient. But something about her, in her eyes; a melting look that melted me, if, all the time we were together, sweet words of love and all of that, I knew it was impossible. I was out of a Glasgow slum, as, sometimes, when we had rows, she was not slow in reminding me. In retaliation I would call her a stuck-up bitch. A few swear words. But for all of that, our differences – the age gap and her husband - strange things happen and it was great; me and her, before; because of the husband, we had to part.

The next I knew, or choose to remember; and I was much richer now for the triangle, I was in Amsterdam. *If you are Going to San Francisco.* It was as big a hit in Amsterdam as it had been in London and, even now, writing this, that song is in my head.

There were women for sure in Amsterdam; for that was me, the man I was. But a faceless bunch of one-night stands for I was drinking heavily. Night and morning and through the night and I still thought there was nothing wrong. This drinking led; as drinking does, to some dangerous predicaments. But I accepted the risks, I must have done; and this wild jaunt, and it was wild okay, went on and on – Barcelona and Madrid, but there were lots of places, cities; Lisbon and Valencia, Gibraltar – before I finally ran out of money.

It was, anyhow, October of the following year, 1968, before I returned to Glasgow. To my mother's new house in Toryglen. Mary was there and old times again, or as much as old times can ever be. You can't catch yesterday, and I suppose we had all changed a little bit. My sister and mother and me. I had gone away without a word and had stayed away for quite a time and must have been a terrible worry to them.

My mother made me promise that I would not go away again, not, that was, without first telling her.

"Don't worry, I won't."

"Do you promise me?"

"I promise you."

It was good to be back. In a way, but in another way it wasn't. Glasgow was dull compared with London, the cities of Europe. I had a notion to go to America, to try my luck in Chicago or New York, but; and what a spendthrift - I had gone through a small fortune – I had no money now to take me to America.

There was little hope of another, such windfall as had presented itself in London. It had been all luck, and that sort of luck does not happen twice. You get one bite at the cherry in this world. Here today and gone tomorrow. But I had had a break and was not complaining. Not a bit, and once again; I had the urge to try to write short stories. This was a strange nag, given my background. A man of letters. I thought to have little chance of becoming one, but I had to try and; to support myself while I did, I thought for a steady job and became a school janitor. I started this job in February 1970, and I would be sweeping school play-yards for the next two years.

***

Mary suggested a pilgrimage to the shrine of St Anne in D'Auray in France.

"Who was St Anne?"

"The mother of Our Lady."

"I didn't know."

"That's obvious."

"Her shrine is in France.?"

"In Brittany."

"I've never been to Brittany."

"Me, neither," Mary said. "We would need to be there on 26 July for the Great Pardon."

"What is the Great Pardon?"

"A special indulgence. It happens only once a year. The promise is that if you sit up all night inside the chapel all your past sins are forgiven."

She had been around a bit herself, my sister, and – she had not seen the greedy Father Gilmartin take the pound note off our mother – if of a religious bent she is no fool. "It seems a bit unfair," She said, "I mean, even a serial murderer would have a clean slate in the morning."

I agreed. "It's an easy way out, but I don't think there will be too many murderers in D'Auray."

"It'll be an adventure if nothing else," Mary said. "And you never know, do you?"

***

A few weeks later we were in Paris, in The Hotel Oliver. Some friend of Mary's had booked us in. It was not a good choice. The streets outside were full of drunks and prostitutes, drug addicts. Hardly suitable stuff for pilgrims. It was already night when we arrived and the only place to eat was a local fried chicken joint. After a meal of sorts, we bought cartons of coffee to drink outside. There were little round tables and plastic chairs and, in a hot sweltering night, it was – it struck me like a hammer - like yesterday once more. Wild times, when I had whopped and hollered with the very best or the very worst of them. A different me. It was preposterous that I should get drunk and whoop and holler now. Or was it? Mistakes can happen, queer turns of mood – I would not be the first man who went back to drinking after ten or twenty or even thirty years of sobriety. Please, St Jude – who else to ask? – keep me sober, away from strong, head-turning drink.

On our way back to the hotel I was accosted by a long-bearded, toothless, drunken beggar and gave him money, some Euros.

"It will go on drink," Mary said.

"But you know that, don't you?"

"I do." We had hardly seen the back of him when another beggar tried to hit me. I shook my head, that I had no more money, and was subjected to abuse. He was a younger, fitter man than the first one had been, and we quickened our step to escape from him, if, in truth, I felt the urge to turn around and punch him on the nose.

"It was because you gave money to the first beggar that you were accosted by the second," Mary said when we were back in our hotel. "I thought you would have known better."

"I can give money to any beggar I want to give money too."

"That second one seemed to disagree."

"Too bad for him."

"I thought you might have struck him."

"I almost did."

"I'm glad you didn't."

"So am I. He's in a bad enough way as it is, without the chance of broken nose."

Mary said he was half my age and big and strong and vicious looking. "He might have broken your nose."

"No," I said and a sudden laugh.

"St Jude would not have let that happen."

The prices in France are pretty hefty. Euros here and Euros there and the one-way train fare from Paris to a place named Auray – where we had booked to stay, because there were no rooms to be had in D'Auray - was far from cheap. We had to book one-way because we were not sure what train we would use on the return journey. Out with that, we were glad to get away from Paris, from the Hotel Oliver, and on to Auray, which proved to be a charming town. There was a tourist information next to the station where we enquired directions to our hotel. It was just round the corner, so we were told; about a hundred metres.

It was a nice, bright day; not too warm, and we began to walk, pulling our wheelie cases. But some mistake, mispronunciation, for we arrived at the wrong hotel. On enquiring where the correct one was, we were offered a lift by a woman in the foyer. This was just as well as it was quiet a way, and it was a delight to meet such a helpful person. Her English was good and we learned that she owned a local fruit shop. Mary told her we had come to

Auray for the Great Pardon in D'Auray, which was a near-by town – about ten miles away, as we would discover – for the Great Pardon, but, to our dismay, she had never heard of it, the Great Pardon.

Our hotel was in a cobbled square in an ancient part of town. It had tables outside and a homely look and the proprietor was a white-haired, genial- looking man who spoke not a word of English. But with a smile and gestures he welcomed us both. Two single rooms. They were actually doubles, so we had plenty of space and both were en-suite, with a bidet to boot.

I have often wondered if British travellers when abroad, and especially in France, make use of bidets? It is not a thing that you might ask of a fellow guest. Not that I care, except for curiosity. It killed the cat, didn't it; and, the bidet thing, I don't suppose I will ever know. No matter. We were pleased with our rooms and the welcome of the white-haired gentleman, who; despite the colour of his hair, was far from old – under forty, I would think.

Mary thought he looked a bit like the old film star Jeff Chandler, who, too, had bragged a head of pure white hair at an early age. "He was married to Esther Williams," she said. "Did you remember her?"

"We're going back a while, aren't we?"

"They were big time in the fifties, Esther and Jeff Chandler."

"I remember them."

"Esther had a good figure, and she was always in a swimming suit." Mary paused a moment. "Jeff was a transvestite."

"But they were in love?"

"They were supposed to be."

"Can a woman love a transvestite?"

"I think so. Why not? They would have a lot in common, wouldn't they?"

"It was big news at the time, when it came out that Jeff dressed up. I think Esther said he had more dresses than her."

Mary laughed. "I read someplace that more guys fancied him than her when he was in drag." We were in a local restaurant, this conversation. Jeff and Esther. A glamorous couple, that for sure. "Jeff turned heads, so they say."

"I don't doubt that, for he was tall for a man, never mind a woman."

After our meal we sat outside for coffee. It was late afternoon and pretty warm, but nothing to compare with Paris. The stultifying heat of the previous night. The Hotel Oliver. It was a bit of a dump and the streets outside were menacing. But you get places like that everywhere, in every city in the world, including Glasgow; and especially Glasgow. I know some Glasgow hotels that, for the toughness of the streets outside, would put the Oliver to shame.

There was, we discovered, five chapels within walking distance of our hotel in Auray. I had, in my travels with Mary, discovered a liking for new chapels as each one is that bit different from the other. It might be a statue of a saint that I had never seen before. The Curie De Ars, or St John Vianney, to give him his proper title. He is huge in France and his statue is in all the chapels, but I had never heard of him until I was in Auray. It is said, and I can well believe it – a glimpse of his statue is all it takes, for a more benevolent pious looking man I have never seen – that he converted hundreds, if not thousands of sinners.

· The French chapels are all beamed roofs and cobbled or slated floors and high, stone, pulpits. This tends to severity. A wrathful God. That one might think twice before they sin. There is a current believe amongst Catholics that the devil, who is always deceitful – he became a serpent in the Garden of Eden, and you can't get much trickier than that – has deceived mankind into believing he no longer exists. But he does not fool the solemn chapels that you see in France. He exists okay, and in no uncertain fashion. It is the impression they lend, as a silent scream of warning. Ashes to ashes, dust to dust. You are never more aware to your own mortality as when in certain French chapels. A heavy, almost gloomy feel; that, in the sphere of things, the mystery of being, all your fears and woes and grand designs are absolutely nothing.

Dreary thoughts. It is better not to dwell on them, but to let things be. How they are. It is impossible to change them, anyhow; and, as those chapels foretell and foretold us long ago, the only sure thing in life is death.

***

The bus service from Auray to D'Auray is practically non-existent, and we had to have the hotel phone a taxi for us. I forget the charge, but like almost everything in France, it was about twice the cost in Britain.

This was on the 24[th]the day before the Great Pardon, but we were both keen to see the cathedral in D'Auray. It was the reason we were in France, in – for it is far from a tourist destination – this part of Brittany. The odd thing was we had met no other pilgrims and, in the hotel, neither the staff nor guests had heard of it. I thought this amazing and said as much to Mary.

"Not everyone is religious," she said.

"But the Great Pardon should be a big thing here."

"I bet when we get to D'Auray it will be."

And so, it was! The streets to the cathedral had been cordoned off, that there was no traffic to distract the pious. This was where St Anne had appeared to a peasant; Yves Nicolazic, and expressed her wish that he should build a chapel. Real or imagined I can sympathise with the plight of Yves, his formidable task, to build a chapel to St Anne.

He was after all a poor man, and it must have seemed impossible. But he persevered and his voice was heard, that a chapel must be built. The Catholic church is full of similar instances. The power of faith. It can move mountains, what bother to build a chapel? I do not know what became of Yves, but I am sure he died a contented man.

The chapel; cathedral, was packed to the gunnels – and we are speaking here of thousands, for it is a vast place – when a mass was said at six o'clock that evening. This, we were to learn, was for the sick, and there were many wheelchairs in view that night. There was, too, sitting directing in front of us, a boy who was mentally impaired. He was aged about ten and was much too heavy and his head too big, out of proportion, but he was lively enough and addicted to crepes. This is a thin, pancake-like delicacy, much favoured in France. The boy was accompanied by two women and, the one I thought to be his mother, was never out of her bag, feeding him crepes. It was astonishing how he wolfed them down. One after the other. I would think about twelve, but it could have been more; until, at last, she appeared to have run out of them. This displeased the boy, who was about to create a scene when the other woman; who must have seen it coming, went into her bag and produced more crepes. There used to be a character named Rab Haw who, because of his appetite, that he would eat you out of house and home, became known as the Glasgow glutton. I never saw Rab Haw in action, but that boy had to run him close. Or even beat him. The gluttony stakes. It was all but unbelievable as the crepes went down his throat. Then, another turn, when the second woman had no crepes left, a third one stepped in to fill the breach. More crepes.! A full bag of them. But she had to be a little too slow in providing them for, a sudden lurch, the boy, snatched her bag and ran away, straight out of the chapel with it.

"I've never ever seen anything like that before?"

Mary said that neither had she. "And he's pretty plump already."

"He'll be as fat as Billy Bunter soon if they keep feeding him crepes." The mass was out and we were sitting in a cafe across from the Cathedral. "We'll be inside there tomorrow night for the Great Pardon," I remarked. "It's a strange one, isn't it?"

"You won't think that if it works."

"But how will I know if it works or not?"

"You won't."

"That's what I mean."

"You've got to have faith sometimes, Thomas."

"I'll find out when I die."

"By then you might have committed more sins."

"But not as many as I have till now."

"I don't doubt that, you're not becoming any younger."

"I sometimes feel like Methuselah." Mary said it was good to believe in something.

"It's moment to moment on this earth."

"I've known that since I was thirteen years old, after what happened to Daddy."

"Then you should pray."

"What if I can't believe?"

"You can still pray."

I sat, smoking. I could no more quit smoking than I could believe in the Catholic faith. But my sister was right, that it was good to believe in something. No, it was great to believe in something. Mary and most of the other pilgrims did not know how blessed they were that they were believers – only a non-believer, a sham like me, could tell them that. In D'Auray, outside the cafe, where Mary said it was her hope that I lived to be a hundred.

"That's good to know."

"You try your best."

"Do you think?"

"Well, you come on pilgrimage with me, and if it wasn't for you, I wouldn't be here, in D'Auray now. You don't think I would have come all this way alone, do you?"

"No, I'm sure you wouldn't – but I like a pilgrimage as much as you do, and I feel the better for it afterwards."

"We've had some laughs on pilgrimage."

"I know." Mary said she had doubts herself, sometimes. "I think everyone does."

"I'm sure they do."

"Then you should just take it as it comes."

"That's what I do." We had tried to phone a taxi to take us back to Auray, but there had been none available, due to all the pilgrims. "We might be here all night," I said.

"I hope not."

There was a group of priests sat at a nearby table, and one of them must have overheard about the taxi thing and offered us a lift to Auray.

"It is on my way," he told us.

"Thank God for that," Mary said.

"We were beginning to think we might be here for the night."

"It is my pleasure." This was one of the things I had noticed about the French, that they were mostly polite and helpful. The ones we had met, anyhow. Even in Paris, outwith the abusive beggar, we had been treated with courtesy. The priest, and he was far from young, in his eighties, assisted Mary from her seat. "After you, madam," he said.

***

The following night was forgiveness night. The Great Pardon. I had more than most in the way of sins to be forgiven. One, perhaps the best thing about the Catholic Church, is that sins can be forgiven. In the confessional by a priest or, as in this instance, if you sit in a chapel all through the night.

The vigil began at eight and would end at six. We, Mary and me, left it until the very last, until about two minutes to eight, before we entered the huge cathedral.

I had thought for a huge attendance, but there was only a couple of hundred, if that, in the vastness of the chapel, where I was glad to see; I truly was, for he was a charming man, the aged priest of the previous night.

"Did you find it long?" Mary asked when it was over.

"Not really. I thought it sort of soothing."

The cafes across the street were already open and busy for the time of morning, but again; as we had been told, it was a day of rejoicing in D'Auray. A problem was that the sky had darkened and the forecast was for rain. Not too much of it, I hoped. The occasion is but once a year and only a rotter would hope for rain. Saying that I know some Catholics who hope for rain, and lashings of it, in Glasgow on the twelve of July. That is the day of the Orange Walk, all flutes and drums and marching bigots that, for sheer hatred, would be hard to beat.

The centre of Glasgow is more or less closed down to accommodate this travesty, and one is well advised to stay away from Glasgow city centre on the night of the day of the Orange Walk.

For what it's worth the authorities were not slow in banning a Catholic counterpart, the Hibernian Walk – another gathering of bigots, people who, most of them, had rarely been inside a chapel – before it became established, got off the ground.

There was no problem this time, early in the morning, in getting a taxi back to Auray, where, in our hotel, we enjoyed a decent breakfast. By then the rain had begun to fall, and I was sad to see it; St Anne's day, the festival, but I had obtained the Great Pardon, and, so it is written, all my past sins had been forgiven.

After breakfast we went to our room for a much-needed sleep, and – or was it my imagination? – I would doubt to have slept so soundly for a very long time.

***

It still raining, a mist-like fall; when we went out for a meal that evening, our last in Auray, for we were returning to Paris the following day, and later that same night would fly back home to Scotland. Mary wanted time in Paris, a walk about, so we put in an order for a taxi and booked a six o'clock morning train.

***

The sun was out and we had a good few hours to explore in Paris. A more agreeable place than it had been last time, in the night; the back streets. The Hotel Oliver. What a dump. We were more in the open this time, the tourist places, which were packed with Japanese who all had cameras and were busy taking pictures. There must be an awful lot of photos in Japan, going by what I saw in Paris. Mary said she had seen some Japanese at mass in Glasgow.

"I haven't."

"When do you go to mass?"

"Not often." In truth it was very rarely. There are many hypocrites, and I did not want to join them. When I had first gone on pilgrimage, I had misgivings about the hypocrite business. Then, after a little; that I was assisting my sister and enjoying them, why not? I was doing no harm, and it was by way of pilgrimage that I had found a devotion to St Jude. I am at a loss to why, but any time when I am troubled, I say a prayer to him.

Wandering thoughts. The man I am, have become. St Jude. The Cathedral in D'Auray to St Anne. She was married – there is a carving of them in D'Auray -to a man named Joachim, who, too, obviously, was closely related to Jesus Christ. It is beyond me: the whole story, that; if it is true, had to be much pre-ordained. Whatever happened to St Joseph? Far better a pilgrim than a student of the scriptures. Mary said it was only once that she had seen Japanese at mass in Glasgow, or anywhere else for that matter.

There is much to see in Paris and a few hours are not

enough. Still, we did our best; the tourist places, before; too soon, we were again in the airport for a flight back home to Glasgow, with, already, another pilgrimage in mind.

***

I had my first short story published while I was working as a school Janitor. I was paid something like twenty pounds for it, which was a couple of week's wages. This was 1971 when you could buy something like eight or ten pints of beer for one pound. You would be looking now, as I write this, to pay four pounds for one pint. Different times and different prices and twenty pounds was, for me, a lot of money in 1971.

At this time, when I sold the story – to a girlie magazine named Escort - I was working in a primary school where the head teacher was a gorgeous blonde whom I had complimented; in an off-hand way, on her rather plump behind.

"How dare you?"

"I'm sorry."

"I should think so."

I had been at this particular school for only a couple of weeks – as a relief man for the regular janitor who had taken sick - when I had this run- in with the headteacher, who made it clear she did not like my admiration. Another woman might have laughed it off, or have even liked the compliment, but she was not another woman and from that day on, from her to me, a high disdain. This was the first in my job as a janitor that I had any problems with a teacher. My bold remark that had caused offence. But it was not that bad and, certainly, she had not been slow in putting me in my place, and it should have ended there, but – and I have to admit that she did have a wonderful arse – she began to pick on me, that I should be doing this or doing that and I began to feel a sort of whipping boy and began to hate the headteacher.

Around this time, I had another piece of writing published, this in the Glasgow Herald's Saturday Extra. The Herald was and is a respected, up-market newspaper, and it was a big thing to be published in it. The writing was an account of the winter I had spent as a navvy working in the Highlands.

DOUBTING THOMAS

This writing came to the attention of one of the teachers in the school who, for she knew my name, asked if I was the author. When I answered yes, that I was, I knew it would, and soon; reach the ears of the head teacher. I should mention that, in this school, it was an all-female staff and that the regular janitor had taken charge of the football side. This had been voluntary on his part, and for a while I had done the same. It was no problem, and I had quite enjoyed it. This, the football, was a couple of afternoons a week and a welcome break from sweeping the playground or changing light bulbs or, simply, keeping out of the way of the headteacher. But it could not go on, and after a little I began to rebel, her; as spitting spite, and all for nothing, or so I thought, every time she saw me. I had not; not by anyone, been treated like that before, and- because it was the only way to get back at her - I refused to supervise the football. This had unhappy consequences. The school side had been going great guns; winning much more than losing, and it was blow to the young footballers that they were now denied their practise, and, in short, they complained to their parents who complained to the head teacher who felt compelled to confront me.

"You are doing this because of a personal dislike."

I shrugged, a little smile – I sometimes smile when I am nervous

"The children shouldn't suffer because you dislike me."

We were in her room, where I had been summoned. A treaty of sorts. Some peace in the school and, for she was young for her job; in her early thirties, it was beneficial for her to get the parents off her back and prove that she was capable.

"Forget about me and think of the children."

Forget about her, what a hope; or no hope, and she was behind her desk and I was standing and of course, my sweet love, I went back on my objection and agreed once more to help out with the football side.

So, truce of a sort. I had, I thought, regained a measure of self-respect and she, for her part, seemed not to scowl at me so fiercely. No, better than that the occasional smile, and I almost collapsed when, one of the mornings - I was brushing the playground – she stopped to say she had enjoyed my writing in the Herald. "Well done," she declared.

I watched her go, walk across the playground; and she really was a picture. The throw of her head, her blond hair. It was long at the back, a tumbling mass that caught and shifted in the early summer sun.

That first short story in the Herald worked wonders for me in the school. I was a bit more then than just the janitor. The head teacher would now stop and speak to me and ask about my writing. Given this encouragement, that she did not hate me anymore, I chanced my hand and asked her for a date. "Are you serious?" she asked.

I said I had never been more serious. "I'd really love to take you out."

"You would?"

"I would."

"Okay."

"Do you mean that?"

"I wouldn't say if I didn't."

This, her; the head teacher, she was a beauty and something else, an indefinable attraction. Something about her that stirred me as no other woman had ever done. Why this was so I do not know, or only that you can't choose who you fall for. This despite an inkling, her and me, that it would come to a sorry end. But, again; I was infatuated, and infatuation can do strange things, like turn one's head. It did mine, and I was as high as a kite when she agreed to go out on a date with me.

We arranged to meet in Kelvinside – it is the student, trendy quarter of Glasgow – where, it would transpire, she had a flat. I had a couple of drinks to help steady me up before we met. This more than unexpected date, for I had fully expected she would knock me back, and who did I think I was? A man in love, that was who, if, initially, I tried to mask, to hide my love away from her, who, it might, I was none too sure, be treating me as a joke.

She was waiting for me, on the street; outside the pub where we were to meet. A big bright smile. "Hello, Thomas."

We went into the lounge bar and so far so good, the surprising head teacher. She was casually dressed in a leather coat and blue jeans and much more relaxed than I had ever known her. She smelled nice too and when I remarked on her perfume, I was told she had bought it in the airport, duty free; when she was going on holiday to the Spanish Island of Ibiza

This opened up the conversation, and I soon discovered she had been accompanied by her boyfriend. "We split up soon afterwards."

"Why was that?"

She said she did not know. "It happens, though; doesn't it?"

"I said I supposed it did."

"You are full of questions, aren't you?"

"I want to get to know you."

"Why do you want to get to know me?

I almost said because I loved her, but caught myself in time. "You interest me."

"I do?"

"You do."

"Why is that?"

"You know why?"

"Because you think I have a nice arse, is that it?"

"Well, you have, haven't you?"

"I don't know. How on earth can I know that.?"

"Then take my word on it."

"You are nothing if not direct," she told me. "Is that not so?"

"I had a drink in me when I said about your arse."

"You have had a drink in you a number of times when you have been on duty in the school, don't think I haven't noticed."

"A few beers."

"A school janitor should not have a few beers, not at work. You must know that."

I said I did, but she was not to worry. "I won't be with you for too much longer."

"No, where are you going?"

"I've found a new job as a security guard in the meat market."

"Why didn't you tell me this before?"

"I don't know."

"Oh, Thomas, I hope it wasn't me, was it?"

"No, it wasn't you. The security job pays better and I'm fed up brushing playgrounds."

"When are you leaving?"

"In a couple of weeks."

"I'm sorry to hear it."

In the pub, and if the other teachers could see us now. "I did not tell a single soul in the school that I was meeting you," she said. "A headteacher is not supposed to date her janitor."

"No, I don't suppose."

"But you are a strange school janitor." She sipped her drink, a vodka and lime. "We were all astonished when your story was published in the Herald."

"So was I, because I didn't think they'd publish it."

"It was a huge achievement for an uneducated man."

I let that go, my education; or lack of it. But it was the writing that had led to this, our sitting in a lounge together. This game, flirt with me; and she had to know, for it was impossible not to know, that I was madly attracted to her.

"Did you go to writing classes?"

"No."

"You just picked it up?"

"I have read a lot of books."

"I see."

She did?

"You are a surprising man, Thomas."

"You are a surprising woman."

"Do you think?"

I said I did, and we were getting on like a house on fire, and I was invited back to her flat for coffee.

This happened to be a Friday and there was no school Saturday, as, I'm sure, when we had made our date, she had been well aware off.

***

"I love you."

"You don't need to say that."

"It is true."

103

"Do you know why you *think* love me?"

"I don't *think* I love you."

"You don't even know me, Thomas."

***

There is no accounting for this state, the in-love business, and you just need to go along with it; what, in my case, was all but hopeless, and, as I had foreseen, would come to a sorry end.

***

Stealing was par for the course in the meat market at that time. Almost everyone was at it, and working in security I could easily double and treble my wages each week. This had been the main attraction – for I had been told about it – when I had applied for the job. A thief in uniform. It made my stealing a whole lot easier and, hell, I had lots of practice, and was good at it, the stealing. This delight of a job; the money it gave me, and I needed money. You do not drink, not the way I drank; and drinking in the morning – there were pubs near the meat market that opened at six, seven in the morning – for nothing.

But I was still young and could hold the drink and there were no mishaps; not, that is, at my work in the meat market.

***

Throughout this time; some eighteen months, I was staying with the head teacher at weekends. On my free nights I would try to write, and I had a friend in the editor of the Herald; who believed more in ability that the old school tie. By then the paper published about eight or nine of my short stories and he was of a mind to send me round the world, writing about the places I'd seen and the people I had met with.

It was not to be. I was so crazily in love with head teacher that, this offer of a lifetime, I turned down flat.

Alistair – or Mr Warren, what his staff called him - was astonished, until, that was, I explained the reason why.

"Do you think it will work out?" he asked.

"I'm not too sure, but I have to try. And if I went away for two or three months, she would surely find another."

"We can keep it on hold."

Alistair was in his forties and very much of the old school tie himself. But we got along, and I liked him and I know that he liked me. But there was nothing, nobody; not Alistair, who – and if he was bemused, he wished me well – could help me in my time of trial, my love for a woman who did not love me.

I did not tell the head teacher about Alistair's offer, because she was the sort of woman to say straight out that I was mad and, and that I got the message, to end it there and then. This in-love business, and what to do if she dumped me?

What she was soon to do – a telephone call! I was in the house and it was near to Christmas and we had a tree and fairy lights and speaking on the phone to her I watched them blinking in and out, off and on, and she asked if I'd been writing.

"No."

There was a pause on the line, then, "I'm marrying

Bob," she told me.

"You are?"

"I am."

Bob had been her old boyfriend, the guy she'd been to Ibiza with. "I thought that you and Bob were finished."

"So did I, but we're back together and this time for good."

"You are?"

"We are."

"When did this happen?"

"He proposed to me last night."

"I meant, when did you and Bob get back together?"

"Three or four weeks ago."

"I see."

"You do?"

"Well, not really; I mean, I thought that you were going with me."

"I was, but it was always Bob I wanted."

"You have got him now, by the sound of things."

"I'm really, really sorry, Thomas."

And that was it. That she was sorry. And I suppose she was, in a way; and glad to get it over with, that she was leaving me.

*****

In Fatima in Portugal Our Lady is said to have appeared to three children in 1917, and, because of that, it has become a shrine, a place of pilgrimage where we had booked to go. The arrangement was that we joined up with some of the other pilgrims inside a chapel hall in Cardonald – where and why I knew where Cardonald was, the Glasgow cat and dog pound in located. Years back, while I was still at school, I had acquired a pup; an affectionate little bundle of fur, from out of that sad place. I say sad, because most of the animals housed in there are eventually put down. Even sadder, for me at least at the age I was, my new found friend was far from well; suffering from distemper, and in less than a week he died on me. That had been fifty or closer to sixty years ago, but I remember it so clearly. The boy I was and my little dog. It had begun to froth at the mouth and hide beneath the table. I had no money and so took it to the people vet, where it was put down. I was distraught at this and would speak to no-one, yet we had been companions for only days, a week at most.

There was a small group in the chapel hall, mostly women; waiting for a hired bus to Edinburgh; where, in the airport, we would meet up with our fellow pilgrims for the flight to Lisbon.

Our spiritual director on this trip was Father Hughie, a small; friendly, energetic man, who was once a White Father, a missionary priest. He afforded a warm welcome, and if I much preferred an independent pilgrimage, it is much easier and all-round cheaper to be part of a group. Travel and accommodation are laid on for you and you have the security of numbers. This is hugely important if you go to, say, the Holy Land where; all clashing cultures and political strife, it would be unwise to go alone.

Father Hughie's early ambition was to be a footballer and play for Glasgow Celtic, and he very nearly did just that. It was a crisis time for Father Hughie when – he had hardy arrived in the seminary – he had heard that Celtic wanted him. "I might not have made it anyhow, with

Celtic," he told me, if I am sure he thought he would have done and become come a famous footballer.

Still, what was football's loss was the church's gain and Father Hughie spent many years in Kenya in a quest for souls, conversions. There was no need for conversions on the pilgrimage, and after tea in the chapel hall the bus arrived and we were on our way to Edinburgh. There is, at least for me; with a group on a pilgrimage, an initial awkwardness. You wonder who your companions are, and; if I did not know it at the time, we had three nuns on the bus. They would prove to be excellent, worldly women. Not a single comment that I; as a singular sinner in their midst, did not partake in Holy Communion. It is one of the reasons I dislike groups, the Holy Communion ceremony. Everyone goes but me, and, at times, I felt out of it and that I should not be there. Mary thought the opposite. "You might be trying despite yourself, that you don't believe a word of it."

I sometimes wondered, and wondered why I had come to enjoy a pilgrimage. Mary was, as I have said, good company; and a pilgrimage gave us focus, a sense of purpose. That and I liked the pomp, the ritual; the try to be good. It makes a change, and a worthwhile one in this world.

Our tour guide, Patrick, was waiting for us in the airport, and much as it had been with Father Hughie, I liked him straight off.

The company; about thirty strong, was on the elderly side, and Mary already knew some of them. A man named Ralph whom she had met at a retreat in Perth. But it was mostly women and, not for the first time, it crossed my mind that the Roman Catholic Church in Scotland is dependent on the fair sex. There would be no pilgrimages; and much fewer masses, if it relied on men. Ralph was a striking looking man, completely bald and strongly built and, old as he was; in his eighties, not a man to be trifled with.

Patrick, for his part, was much younger; hardly fifty and a lean, wiry, build which was just as well, for, his aged company, he had to help to put the baggage on the scales at the airport check-in.

On the plane I was sat beside Ralph, who, and for no apparent reason, mentioned that he had been born on the wrong side of the blanket. I thought this a strange thing to tell a stranger and, on the bus in Portugal, I mentioned it to Mary.

"I've heard it all before," she said.

"You have?"

"I have – Ralph is not a happy man."

"You don't think?"

"I know he's not."

But he was certainly a holy one and in the airport on our arrival remarked that Our Lady had, so far at least, guided us safely on our journey. I agreed with him, for we were both pilgrims, and, in an airport full of people, his simple faith was touching. There had been prayers on the bus between Glasgow and Edinburgh and there were prayers on the bus between Lisbon and Fatima. This is another time when I feel out of touch with my fellow pilgrims. But there is a price to pay for everything and it was the price I paid to be on the bus, travelling with the pious. Communal prayer. The true believers. After the rosary, led by Father Hughie; Patrick invited us to say with him a special prayer for the Holy Souls in purgatory, and this was done with gusto and we were still praying when the bus arrived at our hotel in Fatima.

I was to learn later that Patrick had spent a long time in the Irish army. "But we were never engaged in combat, thank God."

He was forever thanking God for something, and if ever a man was spiritual; as full of grace, I would put up my hand for Patrick.

Our rooms were fine and the hotel was near the Grotto, if, in Fatima; much like Lourdes, all the hotels are near the Grotto. It is the reason why people come to it, what, otherwise, would be a little-known town in Portugal.

The unbeliever might well say that this; to bring prosperity, was why there was a miracle. As ever, with such things; there is no answer, none at all, I chose to keep an open mind.

For most of the pilgrims this was a third or fourth time that they had been in Fatima, and some of them had little money and had to save all year and Patrick was doing good work in organising a pilgrimage at an affordable price. Value for money. I know of some pilgrimages that are far from that, value for money. With Patrick you got a fair deal, and that is saying something if you are into pilgrimages.

Half of the company, old as they were; many in their eighties, were, after being ensconced in their rooms, down praying at the Grotto.

"I wish I had some of their energy," I said to Mary. "It looks like they have lots to spare."

Mary said it was because of their faith, and that the Grotto meant a lot to them.

"But we're here for a week."

"We could be here for a month, and it would make no difference."

And that was true, in Fatima; where, later that night, outside of a shop, we met with Ralph, who was viewing religious objects. He had his eye on a statue of the Virgin that was a good four foot tall, and his worry was that it might be too big to carry home with him.

I suggested he asked Patrick. "He should know."

Patrick would suggest he could buy a much cheaper one

at home.

"I think it's more suited to a chapel than a house," I said to Mary. "But it's up to him."

We had lost Ralph somewhere in the Grotto, where a mass is offered every night. Not that the chapel; it is built of glass, could hold the multitude wanting in, and we had been warned to be there early. But even then, and we were more than early, it was a pew at the back, pressed against a glass wall.

Father Hughie was more fortunate, one of sixteen other priests who; old and young and tall and short and a coal-black African, said mass on the altar. It had a red carpet and was an oval shaped and the mass was said in Spanish.

Mary said it had to be a big thing for Father Hughie to be on the altar in the chapel in the Grotto, and I agreed. "It's a long way from the jungle."

So it went, the mass. A beaming Father Hughie. It was better by far, going by the look of him, than playing football for Glasgow Celtic. After mass there was, as usual; for Catholic shrines, a candle-lit procession. Mary with a lighted candle, and I had one myself. It was dark by now, and following on; a column of candles, singing hymns.

A problem with some, or; more accurately, with most of the holy places, is that they abound with pickpockets, and later that night, I was vexed to discover that one of our group – an aged lady who was by herself, had fallen victim to one.

It was a crying shame, her missing purse – luckily the hotel had held on to her passport - and all her money in it. I had seen her crying at the table of an outside cafe and had wondered what was wrong. The following morning, we had a group whip-round to help her out.

It was at this same outside cafe that I next encountered Ralph. His big bald head was drooping down and all the look of a beaten bulldog. Mary was, as she will; her visits to holy places, searching shops for gifts for friends. So, just myself and Ralph, and I asked if he was okay?

"Not really!"

"What's wrong?"

"Life is strange."

"Tell me about it."

"I will," Ralph said, "if you have the time to listen."

"I have!"

Ralph explained he came from a small town near Aberdeen and that he had been married twice, and that his first wife had been a good time gal. "She dumped me for another man, and dumped her children, too."

"Were the children young?"

"The oldest one was only six." Ralph shook his head in a rueful way. "It took many years to get a divorce from her, that first wife of mine."

"I would have thought if she dumped you a divorce was for the asking."

"I didn't think of asking. I hardly thought to be marrying again and saw no need for a legal action." He had, for a man of his size, a gentle, almost lisping voice. And he was gentle, of that, I am sure; and I would be surprised if he had thrown a single punch in his entire life. "Not," he said, "until I met with a woman who was a widow."

There was no need for me to say a word, for it was clear that my new big friend wished to do the speaking, his life and times and it was a sorry story he had to tell.

From an early age Ralph had felt the call to become a priest, but, and a surprise to him, he was to discover that he had been born out of wedlock, or; as he had put it on the airplane, on the wrong side of the blanket. This was a terrible blow to Ralph, who, at the time, was an altar boy.

"I admired the priest, Father O'Hara, tremendously."

But Father O'Hara could, it seemed, do nothing to help the young Ralph in his quest to try to become a priest.

"Did he confront your mother about this state of affairs?"

Ralph confirmed that he had. "But the damage was already done."

"I take it you were an only child?"

"No, there were two of us, my brother and me, but we had different fathers."

"What did Father O'Hara think of that?"

"He didn't say, other than that I could not become a priest."

"He could have been wrong."

"He wasn't. Not back then. Back then you would have

thought that I was the guilty party."

I shook my head at the wrongness of it. "I think you would have been a wonderful priest."

Ralph thanked me for that, my comment. Then, "My father could have been a murderer for all I know."

"Even if he was, and I'm sure he wasn't; it had nothing to do with you."

Ralph said he hoped his father had been a decent man who had been led astray by his mother. "She was not a bad looking woman."

"He must have been a big, strapping man," I said, "going by the look of you."

"My mother never spoke about him, and I have often wondered if she knew who he was."

Normally, with a man like Ralph; I would have made an excuse and been on my way. But something about the fellow; his hangdog look and pathetic tale held me back to hear him out.

"My mum was called Wee Bella, and she was always going out and was always all done up."

I let that go. "Did you get along with your brother?"

"I did. His name was Bill, and he was wanted to become a boxer."

"Did Bill become a boxer?"

"No, he was in an accident and lost a hand when he fourteen."

"That was awful."

"I don't know what became of Bill, and I often pray for him."

"I hope he's happy, whatever became of him."

Ralph said that he did too. "Bill left the house after our mother took up with a new man, a sort of steady; who was a pretty brutal customer."

"Did he hit you?"

"He hit us all, my mother as well; and he took a good drink too."

"Why did your mother put up with him?"

"Why do I believe in God.?"

"How did you find God?"

"I think that God found me." The day was warm and Ralph's bald head was sheened with sweat. "I went to a catholic school and one of the days we had a visit from Father O'Hara, who was looking for altar boys."

"You volunteered?"

"I did, and it went from there; and it is my faith that has kept me going." This was after his first wife had proved to be a good time gal – Ralph appeared to have a thing about good time girls, or gals as he called them – and had upped and left him high and dry with two young children, a boy and a girl, to raise alone. "It was that or an orphanage, and I couldn't send them to an orphanage."

By now Ralph had become a bricklayer and it was only him and his two children. "I tried my very best with them, my children."

"I'm sure you did."

"We used to say the rosary every night, the three of us." I thought that Ralph was about to cry, speaking about his children. Adam and Winifred. They were without a mother but a good upbringing and they certainly got religion "Christmas was special," he said, and; at that, a big teardrop ran down his face. "I used to leave their presents beside their bed and in the morning, act surprised, that Santa Claus had been." Ralph brushed away his teardrop with a huge hand that had short, thick, stubby fingers. Not the hand of a gentleman, and certainly not a priest – almost all the priests I have encountered have soft, small, as girlish hands – but impressive for its power. It had been this, from the first; on the plane and in the airport, that had impressed me about Ralph, for had seldom met a more powerful-looking man; and not one in his eighties. But how to heal a broken heart, the wrong side of the blanket deal? It had hounded and belittled him, in his eyes anyhow. He had wanted to become a priest, but the church was not for wearing it. Had I been Ralph, this rough treatment, I would have been done with the Catholic church forever.

Not him, though. It would appear he could not live without it. "It was all I had to cling on to."

And cling he did, with his children, who, in time, became young adults, and – was there to be no end to the poor man's grief? – his daughter became a good time gal and ran away with a married man. "She was only sixteen," he said.

"Did you know the man?"

"I did. And I knew his wife – we were in the same parish - and I didn't know where to look."

"It was hardly your fault."

Ralph said perhaps not, but she was his daughter and the whole thing had been a dreadful blow to him. "I knew she was flighty, but I didn't think, not at her age, that she would steal another woman's husband." I said nothing.

"She must have taken after my mother."

"What about Adam," I asked, to shift him away from good time gals. "Is he married?"

"He is gay."

"Then perhaps he should have become a priest."

Ralph frowned at that, an almost scowl. "A priest takes a vow of chastity, and that includes the gay ones."

"Then hopefully that holds them back."

Ralph said he hoped so, but that the Fathers were only human, with human frailty; and that the devil was always lurking and very, very, cunning. I agreed, this man of faith, and shifted our conversation back to his daughter.

"Do you ever see her?" Ralph said no.

"Not since she was sixteen, and she'll be close to sixty now. What to say?

"You said you had a second wife." Ralph allowed himself a wry smile.

"I did. Linda. She had just buried her husband, but it was love at fight sight when we met in chapel at his funeral. I would have married her the very next day if I had not to wait for my divorce and a dispensation. It was out of the question that we lived in sin." He had hardly needed to tell me that.

"The problem was," Ralph went on, "that this took three years, and Linda's health had begun to fail." Not again, another disaster. Linda's health had begun to fail. I could only fear the worst, and it was not long in coming. "After we were finally wed, she died that very night."

***

I kept my distance from Ralph for the remainder of the pilgrimage. The man's story was too much, and Mary agreed. "I listened to a part of it at the retreat in Perth."

"It's not a happy story."

"But I think that he delights in it."

"He might well do, but it's an awful strange delight."

***

The big thing in Fatima, aside from the Grotto, is a visit to the houses where the three young children visionaries had once lived. Lucy (Lucia dos Santos) had been the oldest, aged ten; while her cousins, Francisco and his sister Jacinta Marto, had been nine and seven respectively, when, while playing in a field one day – on Sunday 13th of May 1917 – a beautiful lady had appeared to them and changed their lives forever.

The houses are the same today as when the miracles – for the lady appeared six times in all – took place. Low, stone-walled shacks with wooden floors and wooden beds that are much like Bernadette's in Lourdes.

They are a fair walk uphill from the Grotto where, when it was field, the Lady had appeared.

Patrick had put on taxis for the more infirm of our group. Mary and me had decided to walk, in; I chose to think, the footsteps of the children. How many times had they come this way, young and free; carefree and happy, but not for too much longer. Lucy would soon be in a convent and would remain in a convent until she died aged 96 in 2005. By then both Francisco and Jacinta were long dead, victims of the flu epidemic that had swept through Europe in 1918.

The odd thing, those children; their short lives, they had been told by the Lady that they would not go straight to Heaven.

I could not understand that one, but then again there are many things about the Catholic faith that I do not understand.

***

Our itinerary included a day trip to Lisbon, and, on the bus, we were praying for all, or most of the way, and we would be back in Fatima for more prayers in the evening.

Still, in Lisbon, and, as it were, let off of the leash, it was a welcome break to be alone and no prayers. A walk in normal, sinful streets where we enjoyed a meal and discussed our fellow pilgrims. Mary thought they were a good bunch, and so did I. "But the praying is something else, even for a pilgrimage."

"Fatima, it is a place of prayer."

"I've noticed that."

"It's what a pilgrimage is all about."

"Then the pilgrims won't be disappointed."

"Are you?"

"No, I'm not! I think there is a feeling of goodness about the place."

"I think so, too."

We had a walk around Lisbon, where Celtic had won the European cup in 1967. "Father Hughie might have been in the side."

"In his dreams," Mary said. "You wanted to become a boxer, but nothing ever came of it."

"Father Hughie is a different case. He was almost signed for Celtic."

"Almost is not good enough!"

No, neither it was; is, not for me – my dreams to become a boxer – or for Father Hughie to play for Glasgow Celtic. "He was meant to be a priest," I said.

"We all think we could have been this or that."

"I suppose, but I never thought I would be a pilgrim."

***

Back on the bus it was not long before we said a prayer for the holy souls in purgatory. Where Francisco and Jacinta were, or were supposed to have been – did such a place really exist, as a half-way house; a sort of holding cell before you went to heaven?

After our prayer Father Hughie had us say the rosary, and we were still praying when the bus rolled into Fatima.

***

Two days later our pilgrimage was over, and a night flight back Edinburgh. Patrick was on another flight, I think to Bradford; but before he went a sound handshake and, as is the way in holy circles, he said, "God bless."

Years before, before all this; my pilgrimages, I had an affair with a white witch — the white bit went, so I was to believe; that she was not for casting evil spells — who said she was of the old religion and bided one, "Blessed be."

She would be an old woman now, as I was an elderly man. In the airport departure lounge where Ralph was sitting beside a huge parcel that I could only image was the statue of the Blessed Virgin that I had seen him view in the shop in Fatima. How he had managed to get it through the airline desk and the airport customs, was an almost miracle in itself. But good luck to him — he could do with some, after the life he had endured. On the plane, I was seated beside one of the nuns. She was a reticent sort and we hardly spoke, but I did learn that before her vows she had been a medical student.

The bus was waiting in Edinburgh to take us though to Glasgow, to the chapel in Cardonald. From where, at about one in the morning, we bid farewell to Father Hughie and hailed a taxi to take us home.

***

Charles Dickens began a book, *it was the best of times and the worst of times*, and the winter of 1972-73 was worse time of all for me. I was in a dreadful way and no place to turn and no one to tell – it was impossible to even try to explain my love for the head teacher – and I had lost my job and lost my way and I was drinking heavily.

I had hoped to become old with the head teacher, such folly; for, some flaw in my nature, a serious one, I could not have lived with any woman for any length of time. This is retrospect, what I know now but did not then, when; losing her, I had thought my life was over. I really did and it nearly was, when, late one night and full of drink, I jumped off of a bridge into the river.

This, my high jump; was all on a whim, an impulse. What love can do, for I had not thought of the river until, as all of a sudden, I was in it. The Clyde. It runs though Glasgow and has many bridges crossing it and I was up and over the Stockwell Street one before I even knew it. A whoosh of air, and I hit the water on my side. It was as hard as a road, as falling on to cobblestones. I was wearing a black winter coat that had been buttoned up but had become undone and was billowing out to something like a cape. On the top of the river, while I was sinking under. I had lost my shoes and it was freezing cold and I began to try to swim for I had changed my mind, the suicide game. But a roar in my ears and the shock of the cold – I was almost rigid with the cold – I felt the water wash over my head and I knew that I was sinking.

The panic of this lent me new strength and I kicked with my legs and gained to the surface and discovered that my coat had gone and that, as all of a sudden, I was completely naked. Not a stitch, not even socks, and what a fool; a drunken clown, to find myself as knocking on death's door. There is an old Jewish saying, "Good luck, bad luck, who knows?" I do. Had I jumped in front of a bus I would I would not be writing this. It just happened to have been the river, that was all. But again, such a night; it could have been prayer – my mother and my sister were great prayers – that saw me through, kept me in the world. As for the head teacher, my love for her would change to a complete indifference. Strangely, now; after all the years, I don't regret my affair with her, but she was not worth the river.

The Clyde, from where I jumped; is less than twenty, twenty-five feet deep. Not a long way down, but when you reach the bottom, it is a swamp that drags you under, and for I had sunk again, I was up to my chest in this clinging mud.

Never, not before nor since, have I known such panic. A fight to survive. But the more I struggled to free myself the more I was sunk into the swamp, and what a place to perish in.

***

Home from Fatima in July, I went on holiday with Rosie in August; a couple of weeks to Icmeler in Turkey. A tranquil sea,and the sun was shining. And it was wonderful to be in bed with Rosie again at night. The hotel was good and we had a thoroughly enjoyable, relaxing time.

Turkey is a Muslim country and a call for prayer is heard from the minarets five times a day. Whether it is obeyed or not is an open question, and it had nothing to do with us.

It can be funny too, in Turkey. The Turkish guys, who were all young, in their teens and twenties, were chatting up much older women. I became friendly with one of them, a waiter; who bragged of many conquests in a season, a summer.

"I get presents, too."

"Do you mean money?"

He said he did, I did not doubt to that that after seeing him with his latest conquest, a thin; hunchbacked woman who was in her seventies. He earned his money, that young man. Icmelir runs for miles, into a huge resort called Marmaris; where anything goes, and one of the nights; for so-called entertainment, we went to see a frightful-looking drag queen.

My first surprise was the size of him; a mega male about six foot four and hefty enough to fight Goliath. The show, could you call it that; such a brute of an impersonator, had just begun and he was singing a Tina Turner number. In a long blond wig and a sequined dress. After the song he vanished behind a screen to then reappear in a mini skirt and fishnet tights and the information that he just loved

Turkish men. According to him they were the best studs ever. "And if anyone should know it's me."

It was all so daft, outrageous, our gigantic host in his mini skirt — he had tree-trunk legs and a big fat wobbling behind — that you had to laugh. It was impossible not to laugh, and never more so than when he was dressed up as a drunken nun and a rip in his tights and smoking a cigarette, I was to learn later that this was his favourite act, and going by his audience; new highs of laughter, I don't doubt that. The drunken nun. What a trollop! She had a crush it seemed on a Father Murphy who, one could only hope, would run a mile at her first approach. Not so her Turkish boyfriend, when he was proudly introduced. A man in his twenties who had a big, hooked nose. At the end of the show our pretend- girl was resplendent in a blood-red dress and bowing and bending to a thunderous applause. Some people wanted their photo to be taken with him, and he was more than willing. A big horse-toothed smile that was dazzling in its whiteness. "His boyfriend is a brave man," I remarked to Rosie.

***

There was a coach trip to Ephesus and 'Mary's House' and I was intrigued enough; for I had never heard of it, Mary's House, to suggest that we take it in. "I had thought to know every place of pilgrimage."

"It might not be a place of pilgrimage for Catholics."

The itinerary hinted that Mary, the mother of Jesus, had - after her son died on the cross- fled from a hostile Judea to Ephesus, where; in the house named after her, she had lived with the apostles, Paul and John.

The whole hearsay was contrary to Catholic teaching, where Mary is claimed to have gone body and soul straight up to Heaven. From where this happened, Mary's rising, is a matter for theologians, and there are more than a few of them in the Catholic Church.

It was early morning when we boarded the coach, and the hotel had provided packed lunches for we would not be back till late, missing our evening meal. Our guide was a tall, exceptionally thin, elegant man who introduced himself as Salem, and he advised us that we should relax for it was a long drive to Ephesus.

Mary's House had been revealed to a German nun, Anne Catherine Emmerich, 1774- 1824 - in a dream. This was a long time after the death of Christ and the supposed flight of his mother. To Turkey? At first it had seemed improbable, but a look at the map and one can see that that it not so far and that, in ancient times it could have been as good a place as any.

On the coach. In Turkey with Rosie, who had once taught in St John's primary school in the Gorbals. It was her first posting as a teacher and, so I heard – from the then parish priest, Father Rowan- she had looked like Brigitte Bardot.

Father Rowan is an old man now, in his nineties. But when I first knew him, he was much younger, in his sixties. The good Father – and I mean that – is now in a nursing home, but he has still all his wits about him. A fantastic memory. When I re-introduced him to Rosie, he knew her straight-off, and it had been forty years or more since they had last met.

I have visited Father Rowan – or Canon Rowan, as he is these days - several times and he is, far and away; in every sense, the most complete priest I have ever known.

***

Ephesus today is one vast ruin. The popular walk for tourists is on what was once the main street. It runs though the city end to end, from gate to gate, and chariot tracks and pagan temples and, graphically; the way to an ancient brothel. Some of the paving is slippery, though; and a woman fell and, you could hear the crack, landed on her head. But Ephesus is used to that, broken heads; and it was an almost grave for the apostle Paul, who had to flee for his life after trying to spread the Good News to its inhabitants.

The day was a scorcher and, in one gate and out the other, I was glad to be back on the bus again.

It is not far from Ephesus to Mary's House, but a sheer climb that; in the days of donkey transport, could have been far from easy. A good day's journey, I would think. Or it could have been two, but it was the only place to buy provisions and it is safe to say that without Ephesus there would be no Mary' House.

I have seldom seen a more idyllic place than where the

house is situated; all flowers and trees, and on a glance – that was all it took, a glance - I fully believed that this had been the home of the Blessed Mother.

There is nothing to prove it, not a thing; and it is a shrine to many faiths, with, I would think, a leaning more to the Islam than to Christianity. There were plenty of Muslim visitors, turbaned men and women in veils and long black dresses that; going by the look of them, had to go back to biblical time. The house itself is remarkably, almost miraculously preserved. The only furnishing is a small altar. There are some who say that the present house dates back only to the third century, but I would disagree. The foundations were, it is agreed by all – the so-called experts – laid in the first century, and I would think; whatever changes, more of a renovation nature than a completely new house.

As it is, an almost dream -like dwelling place, stout white walls and spacious rooms that would have afforded privacy and a degree of comfort to Mary and her companions. We know of two, Paul and John, but there could have been more. The house is big enough for, easily, another five, and one would think for a little group of refugees escaping from Judea.

There is no exact date of Mary's arrival to this house, where, so it is said – but not by the Roman Catholic Church – she lived and died and was buried in the grounds near-by aged fifty-six or fifty-eight. Whatever became of St Joseph, her most chaste spouse? Mary's grave has not been found, what; no doubt, will hearten the priests and bishops, the people in Rome, who, by virtue of their very faith, are forbidden to believe this story. They could be right and I am wrong and once again, as is everything in the Catholic Church, it all comes down to the mystery of faith.

The Apostle Paul, as is well known, became something of a missionary and travelled widely – he converted the island of Malta in a couple of weeks – before, finally, the light went out (or in) for him when he died a martyr's death in Rome around 67AD. His fellow apostle, John, lived to be almost one hundred, and died in, or near, the house he had shared with Mary.

Rosie had doubts about the whole story, Mary's House in Turkey, while I was a full believer. So, it goes. One believes and another scoffs, and a biblical scholar is called for here; events and dates, but whatever way I believe –

what I did not before, on the bus to Ephesus – that Mary spent her final years in the house named after her in Turkey, above Ephesus.

***

In the Clyde in the clinging mud and it was sheer panic, this suction – as almost that the mud was live and pulling me down into it, it's foul depths – that lent me the strength to finally pull free This wild night, the worst one I had known; and all by my own hand. But my head was now above the river and, somehow, I managed to get on my back and a sort of float, as a raft, under a black sky that poured with rain.

I had been swept away from the bridge and away from the city, into, as it were, the countryside. The good thing was, if you could call it good, this awful night, I was close to a bank, but the bank looked steep and I was weak, frozen and exhausted. A sort of dizzy, swooning feeling that; as that soon it would all be over. That it was not, I thank St Jude and my sister's prayers, for, really, I should have died that night.

I was eventually beached up under a bridge in a place called Dalmarnock, this about a mile away from the Stockwell Street Bridge. It was a gravelly, sort of sandy shore and there were hundreds of rats, and I was too done in to fight them. It demanded a few sharp bites to stir me into action, that or; my tormentors, I would have been devoured, eaten to a skeleton. Some of the rats were huge, and hugely aggressive and, as exhausted as I had ever been, this new horror spurned me on to climb up the embankment.

The night was black and the rain lashed down and, more out of fright than bravery, I seized a rat and it squealed out as I squeezed it dead and, after that – that I could be as dangerous to them as they were to me – I was left alone, totally naked, battered and bruised and covered in bites.

I could see the road above the bridge and I had come this far I could go on a little further. This fight to survive when, not long before; on the Stockwell Street bridge, I had; I must have done, if only for an instant, hoped to die.

When I finally gained the road, I was violently sick, the vilest spew, as vomiting up the river. On my hands and knees, but I did not care – I was long past caring – and I was unconscious when an ambulance came and took me away.

***

I was in intensive care for the next day or two during which they did not know if I would live or die. My poor mother. I regret that night mostly because of the worry it caused my mother. Could I turn back the clock I would be a model son. Honest and true and a pillar of society. But we can't do that and I have to accept the son I was and the heartache I caused her.

***

Mary gave me a book to read about supposed apparitions in a place named Medjugorje. I had heard it mentioned, and more than mentioned, on my pilgrimages. The book 'Medjugorje: the message' was written by an American named Wayne Weible, who; it would appear, had been a successful business man before, by way of a video lent him by a friend, had become engrossed by what appeared to be miraculous happening in a little-known town in Bosnia.

His book is highly readable, if a bit crackers. Our Lady had appeared, and was appearing to eights visionaries on a regular basis. Weible, who was a Methodist, felt called, that he had to visit Medjugorje. No wonder. While watching the video Our Lady had told him he was hers, so what else could he do?

This I believe, that he believed that Our Lady told him he was hers. In event, much like the saints of olden times, Wayne was overjoyed. He had, for want of a better word, been chosen to champion the happenings in Medjugorje.

This, put briefly – a video seen at his home in Palm Beach in Florida – is the beginning of the book, Wayne Weible's journey to conversion, to become a Catholic; this after he had visited Medjugorje several times and had become convinced to the authenticity of the visions.

When Mary asked what I made of the book I had to say I was impressed, but not convinced in the slightest by it. "There are too many visionaries."

"What do you think about the author, Wayne Weible?"

"He's got a strange name, hasn't he?"

"That's no answer."

"I've never been to Medjugorje."

Mary asked if I would like to go to Medjugorje? "There is a pilgrimage leaving from Glasgow in a few weeks' time."

***

The flight was to Dubrovnik, and on by bus to Medjugorje. As ever, when you are on pilgrimage, we were soon all praying. This about three in morning, but that did not matter; and we were still praying two hours later when, finally; in the dark, we reached Medjugorje.

There were lots of small hotels, or houses; as they are called. These are pretty basic and have been flung together to cope with the influx of pilgrims. In the house we were lodged there was no air conditioning, and – it was August and the heat was brutal – it was soon suffocating.

The bed was a thin mattress on top of wood and as hard as one in a prison cell. There was a shower and a W.C and a crucifix above the bed, or a bare; cemented wall. That was it, together with a broken-down old chest of drawers to put your possessions in. There was no place to hang clothes or anything like that.

For breakfast we had a few stale buns, and the coffee was rotten and I had a few hard words with the manager, who pretended not to understand. But I knew he did and the following morning the buns were fresher, but the coffee was, if anything, even worse.

So, a bad start to our stay in Medjugorje, and, sadly, in the week we were there, it would get no better. Begging hands out everywhere, and, to me at least, much more about money than apparitions. This might sound a harsh judgement, but; and the more I saw of Medjugorje, the more it appeared to be the case. There are many downsides to the place, not least that; to any sane, thinking person, the apparitions are more than doubtful, and all of the messages are much the same. They all begin with *"Dear Children* and go on to say that we should pray. This prompted Pope Francis to remark that Our Lady is not a pillar box, or words to that effect, the; in Medjugorje, repetitive daily messages.

Not that that has had much bearing on the pilgrims,

who; a full army of them, with Mary and me in the company, trekked out to a place name Podbrdo Hill where, we had been told, Our Lady was due to appear. Visualise. Another message. Podbrdo Hill is a fair walk from town and the heat was brutal. But on we went, with, as it were, hope in our hearts, then, when, we gained to the top of Podbrdo Hill, we were told that Our Lady had already been and was now gone, but; we were assured, she would be back again tomorrow. The same time, same place. I was led to believe that she even made home visits to the house of at least one of the visionaries. "It is beyond me," I said to Mary, "the whole thing."

Mary said that all miracles are beyond the human ken.

And there are other people, millions of them, who, too, believed it all; the, to me, in Medjugorje, totally unbelievable.

The legend; and it has become all of that, a legend, began in June 1981 when; so, it is claimed, the Virgin Mary appeared to six young people of both sexes – she would later appear to a further two, both young girls – in the then poverty-stricken rural village of Medjugorje in Bosnia-

Herzegovina. It would prove to be on-going, the visits; with the Virgin appearing almost daily, and sometimes even twice a day, so, anyhow, claimed the visionaries. I have viewed films of these young people; in, seemingly, raptures at a vision, and I have to say they are convincing; worthy, indeed, of Hollywood. The Virgin is said to be beautiful beyond compare, and Croatian in appearance. She is very young, in her late teens; about 5 foot 7 inches tall, and of a slender form. Her eyes are blue and she has a pale complexion. A small white cloud covered her feet and her dress was silver-grey. On her head she had a crown with twelve stars, and her approach was motherly.

***

Medjugorje would appear to consist of one main street, with the chapel; St James, at one end and the bus station at the other. In between it is ramshackle, dirt roads and streets and not one decent, solid building. Most likely it will have changed by now, for this was 2007 – there is no try for chronology in regard to the pilgrimages I write about, more a pick and mix as they come to me – and everything changes and, hopefully; in Medjugorje, a little for the better.

Air-conditioned rooms for one, for; for me, when I was there, it was like sleeping; or trying to sleep on my hard bed, in a baking oven. The food could do with improvement, too, for it was almost non-existent. We were sat at a table with two women who were really, really religious and both of them were fasting. This, I would discover, fasting, is a big thing amongst the pilgrims in Medjugorje, and it might have a bearing on why the non-faster is half-starved.

As neither Mary or me were fasting we found a place near to the chapel where the food was not too bad, and cheap. One good thing about Medjugorje, almost everything is cheap. Ten Euros is, or was, a lot of money in Bosnia. St James Chapel is high and long and narrow, but far from vast; and could not accommodate, not at one time, a fraction of the pilgrims wanting entry. Still, it did its best with several masses several collections – they could easily build another chapel with all the money collected - each and every day.

One of the days, for want of a change; a break away from Medjugorje, we went to the bus station with the idea of a day in Dubrovnik. I had been before, but Mary hadn't;

and, it is all red roofs and picturesque, I thought to show her around. A tall city. The inhabitants of Dubrovnik are the tallest population of any city I have visited. Not that they are the best built. Wide hips and thin narrow shoulders are common place. But and I am over six foot tall, I had felt like a midget when I was there, as a cut-down version of myself. But we could not get a bus to it, and – for I wanted Mary to see Dubrovnik – so had to take a taxi. There are plenty of taxis in Medjugorje, and they all quoted a different price After a bit of haggling I settled for an honest looking guy who offered a round trip with three hours in Dubrovnik, at; I thought, a reasonable charge.

***

Mary was, as I had been, amazed at the height; in general, of the people of Dubrovnik.

"Why do you think they are so tall?"

"I don't have the first idea."

We had a walk about and a bite to eat in an outside cafe above the Adriatic – it was a shimmering blue and lots of yachts - and then, too soon; for Dubrovnik is charming, it was back to Medjugorje.

***

Podbrdo Hill – where the apparitions first occurred – is not too high, but it is steep and dangerous to climb. So far as I am aware there has been no fatalities, and; if that is so, it is an almost miracle. The hill consists of huge, loose; shifting rocks, and when I tried to climb it, I soon gave up, because, in short, I did not want to break my neck. Most of the pilgrims were of a similar mind, and we sat on rocks about eight or ten feet up. It was high enough, or too high, to sit on such a hill. But there were braver spirits; quite a few, who climbed the whole way up and down again, and I could only say good luck to them. They needed it, the luck; for it was, to say the least, foolhardy. One slip, a misplaced foot, and; for some of the rocks were razor sharp, you; should you fall, would be cut to ribbons. I saw one such casualty. A long, lean, monk with a long white beard who gashed his foot wide open. He was in his cassock and open sandals and did not seem to notice. A cut to the bone, six inches long on the left side of his foot. This when he was climbing; going- up and dead- level with me and I had tried to stop him, to draw attention to his foot but he would pay no heed and continued on his way.

As it was, he made it to the top and down again before, finally; his horrific wound — and it was horrific, as bad a cut as I have seen — a spectacular collapse, and what makes people do such things?

We had two peculiar pilgrims in our group. A mother and son who, neither one of them — not as far as I could see — were in any way religious. The son was a thin, hard-looking man in his early thirties. He was seen in the mornings, but that was all; for he took no part in the in the religious side of things. Nor did the mother, for that matter. The house had a sort of porch with tables and chairs and, regardless of the hour, she seemed always to be there. Not, no way; an attractive woman, and she was not healthy either; not at all, for she had cancer of the stomach. She was more than free with this information, and it was why; one would think, in the hope of a cure, she had come to Medjugorje. The son, it seemed; had come along as her companion, but he was very seldom with her. As always, on pilgrimage; we had a priest for spiritual guidance, and it was the talk of our group when he caught the son as he was leaving his room with a prostitute one morning. The son was hardly put out by this and that very same night he had another woman in his room. It happened that his room was next door to mine, and, for the walls were thin; little more than cardboard, I had been well aware that he had company. By then, when he was caught by the priest, this about four days in on our pilgrimage, I was on speaking terms with him, and it had transpired that he was not long out of prison. A two-year stretch for supplying crack cocaine! I have met guys like that all my life and I was far from shocked and have to say that I

liked him, if; needless to say, such brash behaviour, he should not have been on pilgrimage.

***

There were lighted candles and chanting pilgrims and Stations of the Cross each night in the grounds outside the chapel. A lot of the pilgrims were Italian, but there were Americans and Australians too, and a couple; two men from New Zealand. I liked the nights, the Stations of the

Cross, as; afterwards, I felt a sort of solace. A coffee and smoke and a talk with Mary about our fellow pilgrims. She thought the son a 'rum fellow' and, "I don't know why they, his mother and him, are here."

"Neither do I."

"Maybe they are searching to find God."

"They might be."

"But they are not trying too hard to find Him."

"They are not trying at all, I don't think."

We went on to speak of other things; the strange house visits from the Virgin that at least one of the visionaries claimed to receive "It is all so odd, the whole thing; for I have never heard of house calls," I said.

"Me, neither; not before now, that is."

"I would hold my horses about this place."

Mary said that the believers might be right and I was wrong. "Wayne Weible believed; you have read his book."

"I think Wayne Weible was all mixed up."

"He comes across as sincere to me, and in sound mind."

"He is sincere okay, but I don't know about sound mind."

That night, our last in Medjugorje, there was a strange quiet in the room next door. Not a murmur, and I thought the son might be exhausted or had run out of money.

Either way I was hardly caring. I had seen much worse than his activities, if never on a pilgrimage. People tend; and rightly so, to put themselves in their best light on a pilgrimage. Not that guy, and; by now, he was shunned by our group of pilgrims. The mother, for her part, pretended not to know about her son and the prostitutes. This is a side of Medjugorje; the sex business, that would have appeared to have escaped Wayne Weible. I can't think why, for; outwith the chapel and holy places, it is hardly hidden. Perhaps he did not like to say or had been too deep in prayer to notice. Or, for it can happen sometimes, that the obvious evades us. Anyhow, it was a long hot night and no noise next door and, in the morning when I met the son, I was in for a big surprise.

"I saw a lady last night."

"You've been seeing ladies every night."

"This was different."

"How do you mean different?"

"A vision," he said.

"Do you feel okay?" We were standing outside the house, in the relative cool of the early morning. "A guy like you is hardly liable to see a vision."

"That's what I thought, when *She* appeared." He was not put out, anything but. "I could hardly believe my eyes," he said.

"I don't doubt that."

"But you don't believe me, do you?" He had vivid blue eyes and I saw confusion in them. "It is the strangest thing that has ever happened to me."

I said nothing.

"She was the most beautiful woman I've ever seen."

"How old was she?"

"About nineteen, maybe twenty."

"Did you take anything or have anything to drink before this happened?"

"Nothing at all, I was clean and sober."

"Don't you think you should tell the priest?"

"He wouldn't believe me. I'm the lowest of the low, those were his exact words. How can I expect a man like that to believe a word? He would have me committed, if he could."

"You had no woman last night, anyhow – because when you did have women, I could hear you though the wall with them."

"No prostitutes, you mean," the son said. "But I did have a woman visitor, and it was not my imagination."

"What are you going to do about it – I mean, it could do your head in if you're not careful."

"I don't know what I'm going to do, but I don't think it will do my head in. She was not at all alarming, and she smiled to me in a kindly way as though all my sins had been forgiven."

"Did she say anything?"

"Not a word. She didn't need to say a word. I knew she knew I was a sinner, but that somehow, she forgave me."

"I take it you are done with sinning?"

"You think I'm off my trolley, don't you?"

"I wouldn't say that."

"No?"

"Strange things happen."

"Nothing half as strange as this has happened to me before."

"Are you going to tell your mother?"

"No. It would worry her too much. She would think there was something wrong with me, that I was going round the twist."

"You have got to do something."

"Why?"

"I don't know." And neither I did. "But I think most people would."

"How about you?"

"What do you mean, how about me? I saw nothing."

"But if you had?"

"I'd think it over — I wouldn't want to be thought a

crank."

"That's what I was thinking, and nobody would believe me anyhow."

"You can bet on that, that nobody would believe you."

"Then why did you suggest I told the priest?"

"I thought you might have been upset."

"I've never felt more at peace in all my life."

I said that was good. Outside the house in Medjugorje where we were standing, waiting for the bus to take us to the airport. "Are you going to tell your sister?"

"Not if you don't want me to."

The son said that it hardly mattered. "I won't see either one of you again."

"Will this, what happened; change your way of life?"

"It already has. When I get home, I will make a good confession and try to lead a decent life."

When the bus arrived, it was time to go, to leave Medjugorje; and there would be other pilgrims in our beds that very night. They would not know what had gone before, the prostitutes or; for one man at least, a holy vision.

As we were boarding the bus, he pulled me aside. "She wore a crown and stood on a cloud."

"Inside your room she stood on a cloud?"

The son paused for a moment, then: "I know you think I'm crazy," he said. "I'd have thought that you were crazy if it was the other way round." He paused again, as, almost, that he was in two minds before the following. "There were twelve stars above her crown."

***

Out from hospital I recovered by shifts, my night in the river. But I did not stop drinking. I drank even heavier in an attempt to forget the river. What had me in the river. Yet at the end of the day, when I did stop drinking; it was for nothing nearly so dramatic. So it goes, or went for me; and I was not slow in acquiring a new girlfriend. She was younger than me, aged twenty; and I tried to behave, to lay off the drink when I was with her.

This is a trap; a sheer deceit, that many a woman, and I

dare say some men, have fallen into. They believe to have met a kind, good natured person, when the truth is far from that. It might even go, this pretence; depending on the individual, as far as marriage, before the truth is outed. In my case there was no question of marriage, but I wanted to hold on to her and so curtailed my drinking. Two, three years later I could not have managed even that. I would doubt to have even tried, or if I had had been successful, for there is huge difference between attraction and addiction. I went with this girl for a few months, and I think that she had thoughts of marriage, in which event it was a lucky escape for her.

I was back again with a pick and shovel, digging roads. But the work was local, with a district council and much easier than to faraway places on the backs of open lorries. That and, when I could, I was still writing short stories, with, in my head, the thought to write a novel. It was not to be, the novel; for around that time I won a writer's bursary from the Scottish Arts Council on the strength of my short stories. The old Jewish saying – good luck, bad luck, who knows? – comes back to mind for, in short, this bursary was the very worst of luck. Some three weeks after winning it I had lost my girlfriend and was locked up in a Spanish prison. There had been a fight; a serious one, and the prison was in Cadiz in the south of Spain, not far from Gibraltar. I have related at length about this hell hole in my book *A Hurting Business*, so suffice to say it was a grim, hard place; and the language problem, that I knew no Spanish, served to make it even harder. For a time, the first few weeks; for should you want to fast track learning Spanish I can think of no better place than prison. A brisk, harsh lesson. There were a few lessons to be learned in that place. Some of the cons were half mad and one guy thought he was the rightful king of Spain. The problem with such a man, he had murdered five other men, was that you had to play along with him or you might be number six. He was on my landing, in a near-by cell, and we got along okay and when he was released, I was to become a duke. A week or so later; I forget just why, for what reason, I was demoted to a sharecropper. But not for too long, and I was soon back up there as a duke, before, again; for some imagined slight, I was once again a sharecropper. He was as mad as a hatter, but very, very dangerous; and there were other, equally dangerous men and – once again I have to thank St

Jude that I survived that place – it was a day at a time that you came through, survived to see another night.

I was in this place for the best part of two years, and in and out of court several times – they had three judges, all men – but always remanded back to jail, before; for no reason, or none that I could think of, I was called to see the prison boss and simply told that I was released and, I knew him pretty well by then: "Adios, Tomaso."

***

Back in Glasgow I was soon to learn that Alistair Warren had left the Herald on a matter of principle, a dispute with his board. The new editor had his own ideas and it was soon made clear they excluded me. One should take a chance when the chance is there, for chances; such as Alistair's trip, don't come up too often. As it was I had now no market for my stories. Not that I could have made a living out of them, but with Alistair's help, I could have tried my hand at journalism. But Alistair had gone away and that help was not forthcoming and, to stay in writing – short stories are notoriously hard to place - I thought a novel to be my only option.

Writing it was another matter. I was used to short, sharp prose. It is an art, short story writing; if, much like poetry, a neglected one today. A novel on the other hand is more a chore to not compare. A word count! Another problem at that time I was suffering a block. A bad one. I could not put two words to three and, in short, after numerous tries, I thought that I was all washed up, as a writer anyhow. Eventually, though; if I don't know how, I did complete a novel. Word for word it was not my best work, far from it. None the less I sent it out and, some surprise, it caught the interest of a London agent, but; much as he tried, he could not find a publisher. This was about two years on from my time in Spain, and nothing; not one word published, I eventually gave up on it, the writing. Thinking now, for I had recovered from my block, this was a stupid thing to have done, for, with the help of the agent, I was on the verge of breaking though. The world of books. There were, according to him, a couple of publishers who were eager to read my next book. They would have a long wait, for I did not even try to write it. It appeared to me that I did not fit in, that, amongst smart people, I was clumsy and uneducated and socially inadequate in my try to become an author.

At this time, I had a job as a slater's mate, and the slater drank as much as I did. We were employed by a housing association, but there were lots of homers – work done on the side – with individual home owners who required work done on their roofs. It was cash in hand and the cash was spent in pubs. We, the slater and me, were in our thirties and had plans to set up on our own when, one winter day when the roofs were icy, he slipped and fell and smashed his legs so badly that his days on roofs were in the past. This was a blow to both of us, but especially him, who; for all his drinking, had been a tremendous worker, slater of roofs – he needed to be, because you don't drink, not the way he drank, without a healthy income. Not long after this, the injured slater, I packed a bag and went to England.

***

May 28 is the Feast Day – meaning the day of the death of a particular saint, or as close to it as possible – of St Anthony of Padova, in Italy. St Anthony is much loved amongst the faithful, and, should you lose a valuable, then a prayer to him could be the answer that it is successfully restored. There had been a weekly novena to St Anthony in St Francis in Glasgow's Gorbals for many years. It has, because of the closure of St Francis Chapel in 1998, now moved to Blessed Don Dun Scotus; still in the Gorbals and still Franciscan, where it is said each Tuesday night. Mary had been attending this novena since she was in her teens, and; as ever, it was her suggestion that we were in Padova for the saint's feast day. There had been a bit of a screw-up travel wise with this one. We should have flown to Verona or Milan, both of which are near to Padova; rather than, what we did, a flight to Bologna, which is an industrial sort of place; but interesting in its way. The railway station. This would appear to be the red-light district of Bologna, and we were dropped off at it by the airport bus. Mary had booked our hotel on line and it was supposed to be near the railway station; and so, it was, but that first night we took a taxi. The driver took us a long way round, as; no surprise, we would discover in the morning. It is a world-wide thing with taxi drivers to cheat strangers with longer routes. The hotel was a ten-minute walk from the station, but fifteen minutes in the taxi. It was a warm, almost balmy night and, after checking in at the hotel, we found a near-by cafe and relaxed with cups of coffee. Mary said she had been glad to get away from the railway station. "I saw a guy eyeing up my bag."

"You should have told me."

"I hid behind you."

"I didn't notice."

"Well, I did – just before we got the taxi."

"There were a few dodgy looking characters, but I didn't think it was that bad."

"You would have thought it worse than bad if I had had my passport and my money stolen."

"St Anthony would have found them."

"Don't be flippant."

"Then St Anthony would not have let it happen."

Mary said we sometimes had to help St Anthony by looking after our own possessions to the best of our ability.

I agreed, then: "That was some story you told me about

St Anthony and the fishes."

"It's supposed to be true."

"It takes a bit of believing." St Anthony had, so it seemed, been preaching to a lethargic congregation beside a river when; fed up with them, their lethargy, he had announced that the fishes in the river would pay more heed to him, when, as on the moment; leaping up, their heads above the water, the fishes had obviously agreed. "But it makes a good story."

Mary said she had seen an illustration of St Anthony and the fishes in a picture book when she was about ten years old. "But there are people who believe it."

"I don't doubt that." And neither I did, some pilgrims I'd met. "I think I know a few of them".

Mary said we would need to enquire about the train to Milan and from there to Padova. "I don't fancy going back to that station again."

"It will be different in the day time."

"I hope so."

"Wait and see."

And it was, just a normal little railway station. There were, not in the station but near to it, some pathetic looking vagabonds, but; poor unfortunates, they were not of our concern, and the station staff were helpful – especially when they learned that we were going to Padova for St Anthony day – and we bought tickets to travel there the following morning, the 28th.

***

It was easy to know what stop to get off of the tram in Padova because almost all of the passengers alight there. The basilica of St Anthony. It is in a side street that opens up to a cobbled square, and we just followed after them; those good Italian Catholics.

"I never thought," Mary said, "that I would be here, in Padova on St Anthony's day."

"Well, you are."

"I know I am, but it's still hard to credit."

It was even harder for me to credit, that I was there. The way of things, and it was a crooked road that I had travelled to find myself in Italy; in Padova, on this particular special day.

The chapel, St Anthony's; is old and worn, but; all heavy stone, as solid as a rock – it has survived the Crusades to the first man on the moon, and will, I think, still be there on the last day, however near or distant that might be.

We had a walk around the inside of it, but not for nearly as long as I would have liked – it is a place to explore, St Anthony's in Padova – as, outside, there was already a huge crowd waiting for the yearly procession to begin. And when it did it went on and on, as; it seemed to me, the whole population of Padova taking part.

First, we had the dignitaries, all big smiles and benevolent waves, in open-top saloon cars. Following them on foot and marching proudly, were the local police and fire service. And so it went, group after group, all with standards; religious banners of their own, and all in honour of St Anthony.

For safety reasons, this parade; the streets had been cordoned off and you were stuck where you stood until it was all over. That was the plan, as I saw it; on the feast day of St Anthony.

The problem was a threatening sky. This all of a sudden, for the day; till now, had been bright with sunshine, blue skies. Not anymore! A dramatic shift in the sky above and black clouds rolling in. Mary exclaimed, she hoped it didn't rain.

"So do I, but I think it will." And it did, and how; a deluge, the heaviest rainfall I have ever known. A biblical flood, it was nothing less; and it crossed my mind, it truly did, of Noah and his ark. The whole procession in disarray, and the police could not control the crowd, who; one and all, were running for cover and me and Mary with them.

We ended, a whole crowd of us, all soaking wet, under one of the columns in the square, the chapel of St Anthony.

The day had darkened into night and the rain outside, on the cobbles; had become a river, as high as the kerbs, and from out of no -place; as a mirage, a white taxi appeared and I put out my hand for it to stop and Mary could not believe it, when, as out from the flood, we were promptly on our way, back to the railway station. I would doubt the people in the square had thought that the taxi was for hire, on such a day and in such a place and; sometimes, it can pay to be opportunistic.

***

I had thought to go to London, but for whatever reason – I suspect because it was easier to skip the train fare – I ended up in Manchester. Not that it mattered where I went, for I was stuck with myself; the way I was and, in all – for an easier time, with my mother - far better had I stayed in Glasgow. But, all my life; how things worked out, I appeared to choose the hard way, if; of course, not knowingly. I did not know, not then; if I should have done, that there was no escape from my addiction to the bottle, not geographically.

I had been to Alcoholics Anonymous a few times by now, but it had not made much difference. I had met some good guys who, like me, had, or still were, suffering from the pull – and it is all of that, a pull – of insane drinking. We had that in common, if nothing else; but I could not get a grip on it, the message that they preached, a belief– it would appear to be the only salvation, escape from the bottle – in a Higher Power, a God as you understood him. My problem, I believed in no god; so how could I connect with a higher power? The whole Alcoholics Anonymous thing was too much for me, but it was the only place where I could meet with people who were in the same boat as I was.

After years of drinking, I was still; on the physical side, in reasonable shape, but mentally it was another story. The loss of self-respect, the feeling I was worthless. This did not show, not outwardly; for I was good at putting a face on things. In Manchester, where I lived in a cheap bed-sit and, once again, was working on building sites. This time as a bricklayers labourer, a hod-carrier; in that I supplied the bricks to the brickies. You worked as a team at this game, one labourer to two brickies; and you got paid by the number of bricks that were laid, and; if heavy work, it was good money for all three of us. It was a five-day week and it would be safe to say that I was drunk on the Friday night and all-day Saturday before trying to ease off on Sunday.

Sunday night I usually went to AA. One day at a time. I could understand that message, but when it came to the

Friday I would be drinking again, for all; by now, my hangovers were massive. The shakes and sweats, but I could handle them, and it was the worthless feeling; a depression pure and simple, that was really getting to me. On the Friday night, when I started drinking heavily, I could put the kettle on for a depression on the Sunday. This would ease up as the week went on and it suited me to forget about the Sundays, until; that was, I began to drink on Sunday and was in no fit state for work on Monday.

The brickies could not afford to carry an unreliable hod-carrier, so I left the job; or, more accurately, was told to leave. It was no big deal, and a week or so later I moved to Bradford where, so I had been told, there was plenty of building work going on. And so, it proved, and I soon found another job and another bed-sit and I quit on the AA meetings and my drinking went from bad to worse. This was a mean time. In Manchester I had been able to save a little money every week, but not in Bradford. I was next best to a tramp in Bradford and staying in a working men's hostel that was, in effect, a model lodging house. I was a step away, nothing more; from a wine-drinking tramp, a down and out. I escaped that fate, but narrowly. A footloose drunken vagabond. What I was. For a couple of years in my late thirties. What a waste of time, how I see it now; but could not then, caught; as I was, in a blur of alcohol, as imprisoned in a bottle. There have been many books and a few films about alcoholism, but; as they say in AA, you have to walk the walk to talk the talk and every story is that bit different.

I have met men in AA who did not start drinking until well in their forties, fifties – I remember one guy who was almost seventy – and they were all in as bad a way as any other one of us who had been drinking all our lives. Something in their genes, make-up; that they had no tolerance at all for alcohol? The good thing was they had sense enough to try and address the problem. I did not, or only in the most half-hearted way, for; bad as it was, the life I lived, I did not; not in the sum of me, want to give up drinking. Not at that time, and there would be a lot more punishment; years of it, before I knew that I would stop, be done with booze forever.

***

"That was some rain."

"You can say that again."

"It scattered the procession."

"I know. I've never known a quicker clearance."

"But it's stopped now," Mary said, "they might re-assemble."

On the train on the way to Milan, and if the rain had stopped – a thirty-minute downpour – I did not think the procession would re-assemble. "Their clothing will be too wet," I said, "but it was nice while it lasted."

"For about five minutes."

"There's nobody can make the weather."

"At least we were there," Mary said, "in Padova on St Anthony's day."

"I don't think I'll forget it."

"Me, neither."

"The day that the rain came down."

"It surely did," Mary said. "That taxi was a godsend."

***

It was night when we reached Bologna. The painted girls outside the station, as usual. It is a fair bet that they had been there; as in with the bricks, since the station was built. But they were no trouble and, in a way, lent a gaudy glamour. The night was hot and sultry and so were some of them, red pouting lips and the way they stood, as a magnificent defiance. It was what I thought, if I did not say to Mary.

Walking back to our hotel, we stopped again at the near-by cafe for a couple of pizzas and ice cream. After that we ordered coffee and Mary said, for no reason; or none that I could think of: "Do you remember daddy saying the rosary in the house at night?"

"I do."

"We used to make faces to each other when he was saying the rosary."

"I remember."

"That was a good time."

"And so it was, had been. An age of innocence. It was

what I miss most about not having children of my own. Kidding on about Santa Claus and Hallowe'en and, had I had children in my fifties, when I had finally straightened out, I would have delighted in that childhood time and no religion, none at all; not even a baptism.

This would have turned my father in his grave, but that was him and I am me and that is the way it would have been, what was not to be and is hardly likely to happen now when I am in my seventies.

"You remind me of daddy sometimes."

"I can't think why, because daddy was a walking chapel."

Mary said she didn't mean religious-wise. "You are a heathen compared to him."

"I know that, and I also know priests who are heathens compared to him."

"But you look like him at times," she said, "and you walk the same, did you know that?"

"No, I didn't; and I can't remember how he walked."

"The same way as you walk."

"There's bound to be some similarities, he was my father after all."

"He was a proud man, and I often wonder how he felt — being carried off of a bus and onto the road and dying there, amongst strangers."

"This is becoming too morbid," I said. "We have had a good day, and I think that we should leave it there."

Mary agreed. "But I loved him, you know."

"So did I, in a way — we used to play at table tennis on Sunday nights before he began the rosary."

"It was always that, wasn't it; the rosary," Mary said. "From what I heard he was saying the rosary on the instant of his death."

In Bologna. It was late and the cafe was closing. Our talk of the past, our father; of how it had been in our house in the Gorbals long ago. "I hope he went to heaven."

"I'm sure he went to heaven."

***

Some years before, when I had just stopped drinking, I

had gone to a spiritualist meeting in Langside in Glasgow in the company of a woman. She was the reason I was there, at the meeting, where; some thirty of us, we said a prayer before proceeding to our encounter with the spirit world. I was not particularly enamoured with this girl friend, but I was at something of a loose end and she was better than nothing, than sitting alone at home at night, I forget her name, Kathleen or Evelyn; something like that, but I do not forget that meeting.

The spiritualist was a woman from Northern Ireland. She was tall and thin, with long white hair and sharp blue eyes. We, the audience, were sat in pews while she stood in front and closed her eyes and, in a sort of trance, soon made contact with the other side. There was a message or two, so she said; if I did not believe a word of it, from the departed to the living, the people in the room.

A man was advised by a dark-haired female spirit – his wife, he said – to take care of his health or he might soon be joining her.

There were a couple more, rather mundane messages, then: "I have a man with me who breaks big stones with a big, a huge hammer."

I did not know just what to think except I had been wrong, that the spiritualist was no fake. That and I was frightened, a fear of the unknown. What to do? The spiritualist had become intense, as agitated. "I can hear him break the stones." There was a silence in the room, and I wished I was anywhere else but there.

"He has a message for some-one here."

Still a silence in the room.

"I have him with me."

The Catholic Church advises believers not to attend at séances, and if there was ever a Catholic it was my father, which; in a way, made the whole thing stranger, that he was as hovering some place in the room.

"He is a big spirit."

I tried to look as inconspicuous as possible.

The spiritualist had opened her eyes and was looking around the room. "Put up your hand, whoever you are."

I had come to this place for a night out, nothing more; and certainly not this. My father. It was hard to credit, but – wherever he was, in whatever void – his spirit was in that room.

There was no trick in this, the spiritualist; it was impossible for any trick, and going by the look of her; as, in her frustration, as bamboozled as I was by this whole thing, happening – what had never happened to her before – and, saying as much, and that she was now exhausted, she closed the meeting then and there.

Afterwards, when she had recovered – the woman had been very, very upset at what had happened – there were private consultations and I thought to have a word with her, but; for there are some things you should not know, it might be as well that I did not.

***

With Mary in Bologna. Walking back to our hotel. I had said nothing to her about the spiritualist meeting – not a word, and should she read this it will be the first she knows about it - and how our father had tried to contact me. I had and have no doubt at all that it was my father at that meeting, if; try as I might, and I have tried – for in his life, he would have had no time for spiritualists – the whole thing is beyond me. The magician, Houdini, is reported to have exposed spiritualists for frauds, and if he did, I can only say that he did not meet the woman from Northern Ireland. Nor did I, not again; for I had been intrigued enough and a new-found bravery to return to the meeting place in Langside, but she was not there. Nevertheless, there was another spiritualist, and I stayed on for the meeting, but nothing happened. There was no man breaking stones with a big, a huge hammer. I went back again, and again; but still nothing, and when I enquired about the woman from Northern Ireland nobody seemed to know anything about her. Still, I was nothing if not persistent – another bad trait in my make-up, that I will persevere where I wiser man would close the door – and I later learned that she had died soon after her visit to Glasgow.

It was a strange experience of the afterlife I had with her, but – the chronology of this work is something of a problem – I already had had a stranger one that I will come to later.

In the morning, after breakfast; we went back again to the railway station for the bus to return us to the airport.

"It was a good three days," Mary said, "despite the drenching in Padova."

"It was dramatic, the drenching in Padova – I even thought of Noah and his ark, do you know that?"

Mary said that she did not. "How could I have done when you didn't tell me?"

"I'm telling you now."

"I was thinking the same."

"You were?"

"Well, it was a flood."

"It was indeed."

"That taxi was almost miraculous."

"Much more rain and we would have required a boat."

In the airport, waiting for our flight. A short one. Under three hours. I felt happy for Mary, how she had felt; our visit to Padova. In the rain, and it was raining in Glasgow when we got there – but that was not unusual.

***

I moved around a lot in England and worked at many jobs, all unskilled; labouring numbers, and one of the days when I was working as a road sweeper - I had plenty of practise, my job as a school janitor – I found a sort of duffle bag that was crammed with money, used five- and ten-pound notes that, when I counted them amounted to more than seven thousand pounds, which was quite a haul in 1979. Enough and more to change my life and the following day I was back in Glasgow. A man of means. I bought new clothes and shoes and a present for my mother, who was glad to see me home, safe and sound. But not for very long. I had always been a boxing buff, and Roberto Duran, who was something of a hero of mine, was due to fight a guy called Carlos Palomeno in Madison Square Garden in New York in an eliminator to challenge Sugar Ray Leonard for the welterweight championship of the world.

I had been to New York before for big fights. Joe Frazier. My first time in New York I had watched Frazier; who was a fierce fighter, knock out a man named Buster Mathis for the New York version of the world heavyweight title. He would go on, Frazier, to decision Muhammad Ali, again in New York, but I was not there for that fight.

I liked New York. There is, or there was for me, a feeling that anything was possible about the place. That and a shrine to St Jude, if I did not know it at that time. Not that I would have gone there if I had, but thinking now I could have done much worse. In New York. There are three other shrines to St Jude in America. In Chicago and San Francisco and in New Orleans. It is a vast country with many States and many cities, but only four shrines to St Jude.

Duran beat Palomena in a punishing contest. On points. The Garden, which is a huge arena and can hold, I think, twenty thousand people, was a full house and an air of excitement, for the fight was pretty much even money.

How much, in present value, is seven thousand pounds? I forget the cost – if I ever knew it – of my visit to America, but; for I stayed two weeks and did not stint on flights or hotels or night-life, it had to amount to a pretty penny. Not that I grudged a single penny, for it was a good time and how I loved the fight game then and the city of New York.

Yet, too, for all of that, a nag of sorts that it was all wrong the way I lived, that; wherever I went, and I had been in some hovels, I was always looking for a bottle. It had by now a devilish hold, and if I was more than aware of it; especially in the mornings when I was looking for a first drink, I seemed as powerless to stop.

Not, not yet! Despite the life that I had led, I appeared a drunkard. I was hardly falling about the place, and I still had all my marbles. In New York I was a well-dressed, respectful-looking man. In the day-time, anyhow. My nights were spent in Greenwich Village, where there were lots of oddities, and a lot of them were into drugs. I looked on in sympathy, that they could be so foolish and would not as much as smoke a joint. I think that I was scared of drugs because I knew what drink could do, and had already done to me. A raging thirst that could not be quenched. So, I avoided drugs, but I liked the scene in Greenwich Village where almost anything went except for violence.

I remember thinking to visit San Francisco, and I wish I had; to see the place if nothing else, but instead of that I flew back to London. This was a much-changed city from the London of the sixties. A harder edge, and where had all the flowers gone? I stayed for a couple of days and then– I paid the fare this time – boarded the train from Euston to Glasgow Central.

Glasgow had changed too. There were no tenements anymore and while this was good for living standards I felt a nostalgia for the past, the way it had been before. More rough and tumble, but, in the tenements, a camaraderie that was now gone, lost forever. But time moves on and so do people and if I lament of days gone by it might simply be that I was younger, as starting out and full of hope. I was far from that in 1979. As that my best years were behind me. It was how I felt, at that time; and I was only thirty-five. I wish, in passing; writing this, that I was thirty-five again. I would not think that my best years were behind me. But it is all different ages, stages, in this life and you think differently at each one of them.

Back to the changed Glasgow, where the people were brusquer; less friendly than in the fifties and the sixties. That and a huge new Asian population. Almost all of the small shops were now owned by Asians. In the old days if you were short on your rent you might go to a local shopkeeper to help you out, but I would not want to do that now, not in this new Glasgow.

My mother was delighted that I was back from America, for there was no telling that I would be back; and so, to give her, her due, was Mary. She was working as a traffic warden; another new thing, for there had been no traffic wardens in Glasgow in the sixties or early seventies.

I began Around this time I began to go to Saturday night mass with my mother. Off and on. This was the first I had been inside a chapel for many years, since the days of Father Gilmartin. And another change, the mass was said in English. Before then it had always been in Latin. I can well remember that because when I had been about ten years old, I had, at the prompting of my father, tried to become an altar boy and had been badly confused about the Latin, when to ring the altar bell. As a result of this I had, in the kindest way, by a Father Beattie, been told there was an excess of altar boys and that my services were not required. This had been a blow to my father, but I had tried my best and it was not my fault that I was not clever:

Who made you?

God made me.

Why did God make you?

God made me to know him, love Him, and serve Him in this world and forever in the next.

At least I had learned and remembered that, the Catholicism taught at school – and that had pleased my father.

***

Late October. Short days and long nights. St Jude. We, Mary and me, decided on a three-day visit to Rome and to take in the mass to St Jude in the chapel that we had missed last time. That and another visit to Anzio, to the grave of our Uncle Dan. In the railway station Mary asked if I remembered the dog I had tried to rescue the last time we were there, in Rome.

"I do, and I have often wondered what became of it, if it lived or died; because it was a bag of bones and the spirit was beaten out of it."

Mary said that the woman I had given it too would have done her best, and, "She seemed to know what she was doing."

"I was glad to see her, I can tell you that; because I was stuck with the dog and I don't know what I would have done had she not come along."

The weather was not nearly so good this time around, with cloudy skies and a touch of rain. Still, it was an improvement from Glasgow; where the sky was darker and a lot more rain and it was damn cold, too.

Italian buses are strange affairs, or they are to me; and I have yet to pay a fare in Italy. And so, it was in Anzio. On a bus outside the railway station which, I learned, was passing by the British war graves.

Once again, the cemetery was deserted. The young men buried there would be old men now, if, and it was doubtful, old age had not done for them, and long ago at that.

The living and the dead. Does it really matter all that much if you live a little longer, when, for every single one of us, we all must die and are dead for all eternity? Sombre thoughts, and; I would think, if you can, a reason for believing.

Mary said a prayer above the grave, and once again I was impressed by how beautifully kept the graveyard was.

Not a bit of litter nor a cigarette stub - I looked especially for cigarette stubs, for Italy is full of them; but there were none, not that I could see, anywhere in the graveyard. But a grey day; drizzling rain, and - what a difference from last time we were there when the sun was out and the sky was blue - we did not hang around for long before, for I was becoming used to Italian roads, I thumbed a lift back to the station and we were soon on a train returning back to Rome.

***

A novena lasts for nine days. Why for nine I can't say for the simple reason I don't know. I could look it up on a computer, but that I have come this far without such aid I will continue on without it. A rough guide. It was my intention. I have little knowledge in theology for all I have come to love the mass and respect the priests and most, but by no means all, of the Catholic ritual.

I mention the length of a novena because of the petitions to St Jude. He, his statue, was in a side altar of the chapel; again, as ever, in biblical clothes and carrying his little axe or hammer. The altar was grated over, a locked-in

St Jude; but there was a space in the grating to as post in your petition. Poor St Jude. Nine days of petitions, favours to be granted. He is an overworked saint if there was ever one, for thousands of petitions. Desperate cases who had given up on human help, and I remembered the letter of gratitude that I had read in Spanish at his shine in St Margen in Germany's Black Forest. It had hung in my head, that letter; a heartfelt thanks for what could have only been a divine intervention.

The chapel, a small one - it is near the Trevi Fountain, in the heart of Rome, but a blank front door and you could easily walk past it - was, on the final night of the novena, packed to overflowing. Mary was shown to a back pew while I was ushered to a front one. The service of course was in Italian. It was said by an African priest who was fluent in Italian. A tall, slender; elegant man who was not unlike Barak Obama, but much blacker. Obama would have appeared as a white man if he had been standing next to him. But similar sorts, both of them; cool and sure and charismatic.

I liked the priest and so did Mary, who, no surprise to me, remarked that he looked like the former American

President.

I said that I thought so too.

"It's his whole manner", Mary said, "more than looks - he's ten times blacker, isn't he?"

"But they're awfully alike."

"Don't say it."

"I'm saying nothing."

"It's a sheer coincidence."

"I suppose."

"If he was Obama's brother or half-brother then Obama would hardly hide him away, I wouldn't think."

"But he's not."

"I know he's not," Mary said. "He resembles him, that's all."

***

Walking back to our hotel in a drizzling Roman night. It was far from cold, but dreech and miserable none the less. The constant mist-like rain. Mary had said her usual prayers at the altar of St Jude, and - why not? - I had made a small request that, to my surprise, was answered.

It had been a good three days despite the weather. No drama like the last time, the dog in the railways station. We did not visit the Vatican, so I missed the big-nosed pope. I have since been told he has been moved to a less prominent position. What a shame if that is true, for he was a mighty presence. But everything changes, even in Rome; and, for I had looked to see, my book was not in the shops anymore and I wondered when, if ever, I would have a book in the shops again.

***

Muhammad Ali was to fight Larry Holmes for the heavyweight title on January, 1980. This fight was to be shown via closed circuit in a cinema in Glasgow city centre My honest thought was that Ali had no chance, none at all; that he was too old and has taken too many punches in almost all his fights since he had tangled with Joe Frazier in 1973. But then again you could just never tell with Ali. He had stopped George Foreman in Zaire in Africa when some had feared that Foreman, who was a murderous puncher, might well kill him. I had not though that but I had not thought that he would win by knockout either.

I remembered Ali from way back, since he had won a gold medal at light heavyweight at the Rome Olympics in 1960. I had been sixteen then, so you could say that he had been around for the best part of my life. The handsome face and dancing legs and you had a laugh if nothing else at his self-praise and poetry.

It was far from a laugh the night he faced Larry Holmes, who - I had seen Holmes fight in the Garden - was a great champion in his own right. Ali clowned, as was his wont, for the first couple of rounds, but it soon became obvious, and more than obvious, that there was nothing there; no spark, power, and as the rounds went on, he proceeded to take a brutal beating. The fight was stopped, and none too soon, at the close of the eleventh round. A distressed and disfigured Ali. It was the first, in his whole career, that he had been stopped, and; it has been said, that he was suffering from dehydration, I would doubt he knew just where he was.

For me, this fight; the end of Ali as a boxer, was as the

end of an era. He was before the Beatles and lasted for long after them. Holmes had put a stop to it, his career, as, in time, Mike Tyson would put an end to his, Holmes. This is the way for many boxers, that they hang around in the ring too long.

But it was damn sad, the end of Ali; and how that end had come about, as; in public view, an almost crucifixion.

I walked it home from the cinema. About four, five in the morning. In the final moments of the fight Ali had turned away from Holmes and, the whole of his left side open, had taken a ferocious punch, perhaps the hardest of the night – I say night, because it had been no fight – that made him scream and sickened me of boxing. My favourite sport, who had I been kidding? The noble art. What rot. This was savagery, pure and simple; and, in a civilised society, should not have been allowed.

Having said that I would go on to write a book about boxing, for if I had been sickened by a single punch it still had a hold, unholy, on me.

***

Between the Duran fight – Larry Holmes had topped the bill, against a man named Mike Weaver – in June of 1979 and Ali in July 1980, I had gone through something like four thousand pounds. This was something like three years wages at the then going rate for labouring. Against that it was a time to remember, to look back on. A couple more visits to watch boxing in New York and expensive seats for London shows. You could safely say I had had a ball, and I had still a balance in the bank of more than three thousand. The one problem, I was still drinking and all the trouble that booze can bring. Fights and wounds and nights in jail or hospital, and sometimes both, hospital and jail. But even the worst of drunkards can spend only so much on alcohol. It is a cheap addiction, money-wise, in comparison with other drugs, but every bit as dangerous, mood changing.

I knew men who were doing life sentences for murder because of it. So, if, as they say, time is money we can rest assured that it cost them plenty. But those are extreme cases, and the normal drunkard; should there be such a thing as a normal drunkard, will fall ill or suffer an accident – the slater I had worked with – before they lose house and home, which is more than can be said for a gambler. I came late to the gambling game, aged thirty-six. It had just not appealed until, that was, I chanced a wager on a horse and won some thirty pounds. I can't remember why I was in the betting shop, but I can remember the pay-out desk and counting my thirty pounds. A week or so later I was again the bookies and another bet and another win. But only ten pounds this time. It was not enough and I put the money on a six to one shot in the next race. This horse won and I was up sixty pounds. Three bets, three wins. It was enough for me to begin to think I had a flair for horse racing, and I was soon in the bookies almost every day in the hope of winning more. It was not to be.

After my first three wins it seemed impossible to bet a winner. A lot of close things, photo-finishes; that I was beat by a whisker, but I was still beat. I should have chucked it then and written off what money I had lost, but; as is the way in gambling, I wanted to win it back. To this end I began to study form, and I would be out late at night to buy a newspaper for the following days racing. By then I knew all about the different ways of betting. Doubles and trebles and lucky fifteens. A few more, but essentially, they were all the same, that you had to pick the winners. From a triumphant start I could have won a prize for picking losers. And close-priced ones at that. Horses that should have won but did not win. It was frustrating and I was soon down two hundred pounds, or even more. What madness, and I was sober enough when I made the bets, so drink was no excuse. Then, when I was in despair and all but throwing in the towel, I began to win again. The trouble was that I would now need an awful big win, something like a thousand pounds, to level up and call it quits, which was my intention. All this in a very short time, a matter of weeks; and if I won some money in this good-luck spell I soon began to lose it back.

In Glasgow in July, you have what is called the fair fortnight when a lot of people go on holiday. When they finish work, they have three weeks wages to cover this holiday time. By now I had come to know some of my fellow gamblers, amongst them two brothers who, both of them, were due to fly to Spain on holiday with their families. The holidays were pre-booked and paid for and the brothers' wages was supposed to be their spending money. However, that money was now in the bookies till and when they asked him for the price of a drink they were refused. On hearing this I saw fit to treat the brothers to a few beers. They were a likable pair and I almost offered to make good their losses. But almost is nothing, and I don't know if they went on holiday or stayed at home, not that it matters, and, had I given them money, the chances are they would have gambled it away, because the gambler always thinks they are due a turn, that their luck will change.

Gambling is a secret vice, until; that is, should you lose enough, the bailiffs are battering on the door to evict the gambler and his family. Bad as it was, my own gambling never came to that. Inside a couple, three months of it, I learned my lesson with a bet of one hundred pounds on a much-fancied favourite. It was beat on the line and finished me with gambling. I have never bet again and, if I did not think it at the time, it was the very best result for me, that I was finished with gambling before it had done too much damage. I wish I had quit on the drinking game so sharply, but it was not to be, not; that is, before almost forty years of punishment

***

By now, after the gambling; out of the original seven thousand pounds I had less than eight hundred left. It was enough for a holiday, and I flew to London and on to Morocco, which was a random choice if there was ever one.

In the Gorbals in the fifties Father Gilmartin had two curates, Father Beattie and Father Cunningham. My father, who was a pass keeper – this meant that he helped put round the collection box amongst the congregation – was friendly with Father Beattie, who had been an army chaplain. He was a soft spoken, taciturn man in, I would think, his forties. Now and again, he would visit the house and my mother would fuss over him and my father would feel that he was be blessed. A man in dark clothes who wore a tight white collar. It did a lot, that collar did; in my household, anyway.

The other priest, Father Cunningham, was much younger, in his mid-twenties and newly ordained. I remember he had a gold side tooth and a good head of hair, black and thick and curling. He had a ready smile and the nickname Cherub and was easily the most popular of the three priests in the parish. The chapel was as squeezed in by the tenements and was opposite a ragstore. But, inside of it, there was a plush red altar and stained-glass windows and it was hard to imagine the squalor outside. This oasis of peace and piety, Father Gilmartin and his curates. They employed a housekeeper and a cook and a butchers van was seen regularly at the side door, so you can take it that they ate well and were not short of comforts, other than the obvious, that they had taken a vow of chastity. Along with being the most popular, Father Cunningham was by far the best preacher of the three. That, and that he was young and newly ordained might have lent to his popularity. But, and even me, young as I was; aged ten or eleven, liked to listen to Father Cunningham who, one thing for sure, could tell a story if nothing else.

At the age we were at that time Mary had her own pals and I had mine and, out with our nightly rosary, we were seldom in each other's company. So, it is a bit of a mystery how it came about that we ganged up as thieves. For a time, during the summer holidays. Six weeks off school, and it was her idea that we became spam stealers. We would take turns about to go inside a grocery shop and order up a weight of spam that, once it was sliced and wrapped and, in our hand, we would run straight out the door. It was all a laugh; surprised shopkeepers, and we were all over the place, for you could not hit the same shop twice, and Mary proved to be as good at running as Father Cunningham was at preaching

There was the occasional close thing, chasing shopkeepers; but most of them, their vanishing spam, were too surprised; as taken aback, to even think to leap over their counter and run after us. Many of them were too old to even dream to leap over their counter and run after us. So, it was easy enough, for we were both quick, young and nimble. Then, one of the days, in a place named Polmadie, which was not too far from where we stayed, we chanced to rob an Indian. Or he could have been a Pakistani, for all I know. A man with a big black beard and a big white turban. It was my turn to order the spam and Mary stood outside the shop. The idea was she would trip up the shopkeeper if they tried to pursue, to retrieve their spam.

I was a little dubious about the Indian or Pakistani, who was far from old and looked to be fit enough. He was careful about weighing the spam to an exact amount. His hands looked big and were covered with thick, black hair. But there was no way now I could get out of it, except, as planned, to snatch the spam and run away. What I did, with him up over his counter and hot on my tail.

Where Mary was, I did not know, and had no time to look and see, not with the enraged Indian or Pakistani – he had to have been one of the first Asian shopkeepers in Glasgow – screaming out in a strange tongue and chasing after me.

I ducked through a close and over a backcourt where I scaled a wall, but he was still there as to show his grit that there was nobody going to steal from him. This is a trait with Asian shopkeepers, who, some of them, would risk their life to save a pound. My pursuer was of that mould, and I thought he meant to kill me. I truly did, such a chase; through closes and backcourts and over walls, all for a measure of spam.

This chase had had to go on five minutes, which is a long time when you are being chased. At one point I had thought to stop and face up to him, that or beg; plead for mercy, but on I ran, and; one thing for sure, I would not be stealing spam or anything else from his shop again.

By now we were on the open road, going towards St Bonaventures. I was flat out and the shopkeeper not far behind. He wore a sort of skirt and baggy white trousers and I would doubt to have run so fast in all my life till them. On the road, and I could now see St Bonaventures. Father Cunningham. It was his habit to sometimes stand outside the chapel for a smoke. His gold side tooth. It is the thing I remember best about Father Cunningham, that he had a gold side tooth. That and a sense to protect his flock, and, "Run like the devil," he told me as I sped past him. It was the end of the chase, for Father Cunningham tripped up the shopkeeper and, afterwards, when I saw him, he winked to me and that was all. Run like the devil. It is an odd expression, and Father Cunningham would soon have his own personal encounter with the evil one. It was the talk of the place; the tenements, for Father Cunningham was far from loath in recounting his adventure from the pulpit. I sat enthralled, listening, for, as said, he could tell a story, or, in this case, a happening to him.

From what I gathered he had been summoned to a sick

call where the victim was dying. Father Cunningham went with his sacraments; the last rites, for, should a sinner repent, he will be forgiven. Something like that, that; by luck or whatever, he would certainly not go to hell. Should hell exist. I don't think so. Such a place, an eternity in a hot — to say the least — torture chamber does not fit in with a loving god. But the Catholic church believes in it, and the devil; and so, did Father Cunningham, especially the devil. No sooner had he entered the house than the sick man shook; a tremendous death rattle, and on the instant the devil called to collect his prize. A loud villainous laugh and it was icy cold and the body lifted up a good foot off the bed. Father Cunningham felt his hair stand on end and fled the house, reciting the Lord's prayer over and over. When he gained the street — the house had been top-landing in a tenement — Father Cunningham tried to compose himself, but it was useless. A brisk walk became a trot to an outright run back to the chapel where he threw himself on the altar, below the blessed Sacrament.

This story became something of a legend, and people wondered who the dead man was, but so far as I know no-one found out, or if they did, they kept it to themselves.

Some sixty years later, in Lourdes, I happened to meet with pilgrims who had known Father Cunningham in their parish – St Bonaventures had closed in 1992, and Father Cunningham had been long gone by then – in much more recent times and they too knew of his encounter with the devil. "He had the fright of his life," I was told. "The dead body moved up off of the bed."

"When did he say this happened?"

"In the fifties, when he was a young priest in the Gorbals."

"Do you remember it?" I asked Mary.

"It would be hard to forget it."

"It was a long time ago."

"Father Cunningham repeated it almost word for word from what I gather."

"It must have had a big effect on him, after all that time."

"I think it would have a big effect on any priest, for a thing like that to happen to him."

"Do you think it did?"

"I don't see why he would say it did if it hadn't."

I suggested imagination. "The mind can play strange tricks, you know."

Mary said that it must be awful to be me. "You can't believe a single thing without rock-solid evidence."

"I didn't comment, one way or the other."

"You more or less said that Father Cunningham imagined it."

"He might have done. I wasn't there, so I don't know. But whatever happened, if only in his head, it had a lasting effect on him."

"Do you remember he tripped up the shopkeeper who was chasing after you?"

"I'll never forget it. I was terrified. Father Cunningham told me to run like the devil."

"Father Cunningham ran like the devil away from the devil after he encountered him."

"So, it would seem. And he was a bit of a fatty, Father Cunningham."

"He was not that fat."

"Chubby, then."

"There were lots of lassies who fancied Father Cunningham."

"You didn't, did you?"

"No. I never fancied him one bit. I always thought he was too full of himself. But Betty O'Hara and some of the other lassies fancied him like mad."

"I didn't know."

"How do you think he got his nickname, Cherub?"

"I thought because he was saintly."

"I am sure he was, but he liked to tease the lassies."

"I would have thought it to have been the other way round, that the lassies were teasing Father Cunningham."

"Some of them might have done, out of devilry – but from what I remember it was more Father Cunningham who teased them, that he was a man they could not get."

"I would hope so, that he was a man they could not get."

"But he did flirt. He was young and he attracted young people, boys as well as girls – but it was the girls who dubbed him Cherub."

I thought Father Cunningham, who was short and stocky and, still in his twenties, far from slim, to have been an unlikely object for the attraction of teenage girls. "He used to run the parish football side," I said, "and he was highly thought off amongst the boys."

"He was even higher thought off amongst the girls."

"That's amazing."

"He might have had sex appeal," Mary said, "for he was certainly well fancied."

"He must have had something, if some of the lassies were nuts about him."

"Betty O'Hara."

"Who else?"

"Lizzie Duggan and Sally Sullivan."

"I used to think she was dead sexy, Sally Sullivan."

"She was mad about him."

I shook my head. "I always thought he was just a wee fat man."

"Still, he saved you when you stole the spam," Mary said. "That turbaned guy was meaning business, and he might have caught you had Father Cunningham not tripped him up."

I had to admit that was true. "But we were speaking about Father Cunningham and the devil."

"You don't believe he met the devil."

"Do you?"

"If he only thought he did, that was bad enough."

I agreed. Father Cunningham. His gold side tooth. It's funny how you remember a thing like that, a gold side tooth, and; for what it's worth, the pilgrims in Lourdes had no doubt that Father Cunningham, who had lived into his eighties, had once, many years before, shared a room with a dead man and the devil who had come to collect a soul and mock the priest while he was about it.

***

Agadir in Morocco was a dump of a place in 1981, and rife with corruption. Greedy Arabs up for anything and the few white men that I encountered were none too upright either. This was a pity as the setting was great, a huge sandy beach and the blue Atlantic. But you had no peace to enjoy the view because there was always someone accosting you, wanting money. One of the days while sitting at a beachside cafe I was approached by a boy in his teens. His opening gambit was to ask for a cigarette, then: "Do you like Morocco?"

I said I did and my young friend smiled. He had good clean white teeth and looked to be clean enough himself. He was dressed in shorts and wore a blue shirt that was open to his naval. I was drinking beer and some sort of spirit, and I had already drunk a number of them – I must have done, or I would have chased the boys away. As it was his company; and he spoke not too-bad English, was better than no company and I was curious to what his pitch would be.

"I am Abdulla."

"I am Thomas."

It would be hard to beat an Arab for instant friendship, but beware. Keep an eye on your wallet and your watch –

which Abdulla was looking at, my watch. "I like it," he said. I told him that so did I and that I meant to keep it. Abdulla smiled. Smoked. The day was hot and we sat in the shade of a canvas awing. "I would like to go to America," he told me.

"But you don't have the money to get there?"

Abdulla shook his head, sadly; that what I had said was all too true: that he had no money. I asked what he did, worked at; and was told he was a student.

"How old are you, Abdullah?"

"Seventeen".

He looked younger than that to me, about fourteen; if that, but he had an engaging way and was good company. Saying that, I was well aware there would be a catch, and it was not long in coming. "Would you like a good time?"

"How do you mean, a good time?"

"Rumpy-pumpy"

"Who with?"

"Me." He smiled again, and I almost laughed. I had expected his sister or something like that. A local brothel.

"You like me, yes?"

"Sure," I said, "but not that way, because I'm not into boys."

"You might like."

I shook my head. A smile. Not nearly as bright as his smile. Half of my teeth had been smashed out and I wore a plate. This was long before implants had become quite common. It was before mobile phones or the internet, come to that. How times change but human nature remains the same. The sins of the flesh, but it was not my thing. The eager young Abdulla. "This is a new one to me," I told him.

"All white men like rumpy-pumpy with a boy when they are in Morocco."

"Then I must be the odd one out."

"A younger boy?" he asked me.

"No boy at all," I told him, and he asked me why; if I disliked boys, I was in Morocco?

"For the sun."

"I have no money."

"You might find another man."

"I like you."

"No, you don't – you only want my money."

"My old mother has nothing to eat," he said.

I thought, going by the age of him, that his mother could not be all that old, but it was a good enough try to get some money out of me. And I think he knew I would give him something. He had, if nothing else – and I was far from offended by his proposal – amused me greatly. It is the ridiculous, sometimes, that appeals to me, my sense of humour. An Arab street boy! Rumpy-pumpy. "How much would it have cost?" I asked.

"For rumpy-pumpy?"

"What else?"

He mentioned a figure, too much I was sure and I told him to come again. At this, and a look at me, he quoted another, much lesser sum. But only because, so he said, that I was big and strong and handsome. I said I would give him half the money, something like four or five pounds, because I wanted to help his old mother. This delighted Abdullah, who planted a big kiss on my cheek and took the money – the easiest money he ever made, I'd warrant – and that was that, an afternoon in Agadir in Morocco.

That same day, or it could have been the following one, I was bitten by a performing snake when walking in a bazaar. The attack was sudden, unprovoked and unexpected – the snake had been up out of its basket, swaying; as in a trance, listening to its owner's flute – and I must admit that I howled in pain when it sunk its fangs into my leg, just above my ankle.

The man with the flute was full of apologies, and nothing like that had happened before. I felt to wring his neck that it had happened now; but a crowd had gathered and after assurances that the snake had been rendered harmless, I had little option but to walk, or hobble away. To try to forget the thing I had a drink at some bar or other. I felt to be due a drink after what had happened. Another, wiser man would have been seeking medical attention after such an incident. But I was not a very wise man, not where alcohol was concerned, and I continued to drink and the snake bite was soon forgotten.

But not for long, for the next day my ankle was

throbbing and my foot had swollen up to twice its size. I was staying in a cheap, but well-run hotel that had a round the clock reception and a doorman named Akeel. He was a big, bald, discreet man – discreet, that is, should you want some company in your room. A word in his ear and Akeel would arrange it all, for a price. Everything, it appeared to me, in Morocco, was for the asking for a price. Not that I cared, and I was far from an innocent in such matters. But I valued Akeel for advice and so rang reception and asked for him to be sent up to my room. One look at my foot and Akeel said he would call in a doctor.

I disagreed, and explained to him that I would give it a day or two in the hope that it cleared up. Akeel opinionated that I was wrong and that I should see a doctor straight away, but – and I already had had a couple of dealings with the guy – it was my limb and up to me and I went out for more drink, wearing a huge felt slipper on my swollen foot. What a clown! There was no way, and I knew it – but I wanted drink, pure and simple – that my foot would heal without a doctor. It demanded assistance that I got back to the hotel, where I fell into a drunken sleep. In the morning my foot was worse, and not only my foot, but the bite itself; above my ankle, was now a frightful sore oozing pus. But still I chose to let it go and another drunken night. In Morocco where, finally, when I saw a doctor, he had me into hospital and, after a consultation with other doctors, I was told I needed an amputation from just above my knee.

When I would not have that, I was informed that I would soon become delirious before I finally expired. The hospital was a grim place and grim doctors and I was a grim man. I did not want to lose my leg, and asked about antibiotics. The head doctor, a man who appeared to know his stuff; if I thought he was a bit on the hasty side, agreed to try them, but; really, at this stage, and even with an amputation, it was a case of Inshallah. Or St Jude. The more I think of my past life the more I think I should thank St Jude. This second time I should have died, but, obviously, I am still here. On my own two feet. I could go on, other near things, but enough I think my night in the Clyde and then in the hospital in Morocco where I was supposed to become delirious before I passed away. My belief in St Jude is the oddest of things, but once again; as throughout this work, we are back again with the mystery of faith.

I was in hospital for a couple of weeks, and it was lucky for me that; with some foresight, that something was bound to happen, I had taken out travel insurance. I would have been kicked out of the hospital in short order to die on the street without it. That was the way it was back then, and still might be for the traveller in Morocco. As it was, when I was half way fit – I still have the scar of the snake bite - I was ambulanced to the airport and put aboard a flight to London and, still in a wheelchair, on from there to Glasgow.

***

"The little flower," Mary said. "It is what they call St Teresa."

"Of Avila?"

"No, of Lisieux."

"Where is Lisieux?"

"In Normandy in France."

It was mid-September and, out with a visit to a local chapel; St Jude's in Balornock in Glasgow's east end, we had no plans for a pilgrimage that year.

This all changed with St Teresa, for Mary had found a pilgrimage; an overland one, that was departing on October 30, to be in Lisieux for St Teresa's feast day on the first of October. The price was more than reasonable, indeed; for a pilgrimage, it was surprisingly good value, and we both agreed to make a booking.

The coach left from outside a chapel in Coatbridge; which is nearer to Hamilton than to Glasgow, in the early hours; something like three in the morning, and in the taxi going there I wished I was in bed. This trip to France, to Normandy, for a saint I had never heard off. The little flower, St Teresa had as opened herself to God as a flower opens to the sun and that; as all-embracing love, was why she was referred to as a flower. In the sun, in her youth. She was never old, St Teresa.

A short, but pious; eventful life. She had written a book - which I read before our pilgrimage – and had entered a convent aged fifteen. This was, and is, a very young age to become a nun, if, of necessity, still a novice. Not that there was ever any question about her calling, and, in time, she took full vows – this all before she was twenty-five, when some might say the Lord called her and she departed from this earth. On the bus on a cold, dark morning. A short prayer for a successful pilgrimage. We were due an overnight stop in Cambridge, which is not too far from the English Channel; but a long, long way from Glasgow. The bus was full, not one empty seat, and I was to learn that the parish ran the pilgrimage every second year and that it was very popular. Mary and me had got cancellations. Two single rooms. There was a small supplement, as ever; another bit of profit, for there are lots of single people, mostly women, who go on pilgrimage. I would fancy they feel safer in such a company. A feeling of togetherness. The priest, I forget his name; if that is I ever knew it, was an elderly, unassuming man who was not too big on saying prayers and after a time you; or I did, forgot that he was even there.

On the bus. It was a modern, luxury affair and, out with the early rise, it was no hardship and there were lots of stops and the time went quickly and about six at night we arrived at our hotel in Cambridge. After our meal, a good one, Mary decided to have an early night and, for it was a nice clear night, I decided on a walk about. I was well-used to night-time streets and being alone, unfortunately.

However, that night I was not to alone for long for I had barely left the hotel when a woman walked past me and then turned round and, "Is your name Tam?" she asked me.

"It is." She was about my own age and vaguely familiar. At the mouth, her eyes. "Do I know you?"

"I think perhaps you used to know me." At that she smiled and it all came back, a girl I had once been mad about. "Brenda Kane," I said, a statement. "This is a turn up for the books." Then. "We nearly missed each other."

"You nearly missed me, you mean."

"My God, Brenda; I don't know what to say."

"No wonder. It must be fifty years, or even more since you last spoke to me." Brenda paused. "I knew you by your walk," she said.

"After all this time."

"Some things don't change – the way you walk, for instance."

"It must be the only thing about me that's not changed."

"How are you doing, Tam?"

"I'm okay, but how about you? I want to know all about you, Brenda."

"My car's just across the road," she said, and took my arm and we crossed the road, towards her car. "It's the strangest thing, meeting you again."

"How do you think I feel?" But I felt at ease; as, in a way, it was like yesterday once more. There was no awkwardness at all with her, this girl I used to know. In the tenements, the gas-lit streets. It was a world from Canterbury, or present-day Glasgow for that matter. A more primitive time, as I have tried to explain; but I have not explained, nor tried to explain Brenda Kane and the effect she had on me. On a glance, it was all it took; much the same as it had been with Judith and the head teacher and one or two others, who, my hasty heart, a lover in love, had all but finished me.

***

The strange thing, I had known Brenda – she had stayed in the next close to me – all my life but had never really noticed her until, one summer morning on the street, I saw her ride a bike. In a circle, round and round, an easy grace; all trim and neat and the sun in her hair, and, on the instant, she was nothing less than beautiful, wonderful to me. I was fourteen years old and had already been to London, so I was far from innocent. But I was still in awe of Brenda and the reputation that she had. She hung around with tough, older boys; some in their early twenties, and I had despaired to ever win her. So it began, and suddenly; my chasing after Brenda, who, and soon, that I was always there or thereabouts, began to tease and flirt with me, sometimes quite outrageously.

This, my thing with Brenda; an unreal fascination, attraction, was during the school holidays in the summer of 1958. I remember a first interest in boxing and that Floyd Patterson was the heavyweight champion. I admired him, but nothing nearly as to how I admired Brenda. How she was, young and free, a rare defiance, yet, too, and all the time, or so I thought, a certain softness, femininity, that no-one could see but me. When I began to write, or try to write, she was a much-used theme in my short stories, the tremendous crush I had on her.

"I thought you had a loose screw," she told me, in her car in Cambridge. "That guy you tackled when we were young was one tough cookie."

And I suppose he was, had been; and he was certainly tough with her all right, and, late one night, I saw him punch her on the head when they were underneath a gas lamp.

There was nobody there but me and them and, for I loved her so, I was not for standing watching it, him beating up on Brenda. "You had a sore face afterwards, remember?"

"It was not that bad."

"He was too big for you."

"I suppose he was, but I tried my best."

"You did, and I was proud that you stuck up for me, but he was still too big and he beat you in the end."

"It was worth the beating, from what I remember."

Brenda laughed. "I'm glad you thought so."

"I still think so."

We were stopped at lights and Brenda asked. "What are

you doing in Cambridge, Tam?"

"I'm on my way to France on a pilgrimage."

"Do you mean like a holy journey?"

I said I did. "But I'm not a holy Willie, so don't think that." She wore a short black skirt and I put my hand on her knee. "I'll never forget that night, Brenda."

Brenda said she had thought I was brave. "No other guy had ever stuck up for me before."

"That was because I fancied you."

"I know."

"You must have known I fancied you long before that night."

"I did, and I went out of my way to tease you – but after that night when you had a sore face, I stopped all that, and you remember what happened, don't you?"

I could never forget it, what happened that night, and it can sometimes pay to be a little crackers. She had asked me if I was okay and I said I was and we went inside a close where rats were running everywhere and I told her that I loved her.

"But you want your hole, don't you?" she asked.

She had a romantic way, had Brenda.

***

"What would you like to drink, Tam?"

"A black coffee would do me fine."

"I thought for something a wee bit stronger."

"No, only coffee; I quit drinking years ago." Her house was a nice bungalow in an affluent suburb. "It looks like you have got on," I said.

"I had good luck."

"I was bad luck for me when you went to London. You told me the night before, I think. That you had a new boyfriend, Big Andy, and you were going to London with him."

Brenda said she had been only sixteen and, "He was a waste of space, Big Andy."

"So, it didn't work out?"

"It did not, not for me; I was a prostitute within a

week."

It had been on the cards, a girl like her, that; and in a city such as London, she would become a prostitute. It was the one sure way to make some money, to please Big Andy and survive. This went on for a couple of years, until Big Andy had murdered someone and had been sent to prison. "It was a whole new freedom," she told me, "And shortly after I met Henry." Henry was an older man, in his late thirties; and well set-up financially. He had had no idea what Brenda did and she was not about to tell him. "Would you?"

"No, I'd not have said a dicky bird."

"I told him I was a shop assistant, and played hard to get." We were seated together on a couch, both of us smoking and Brenda sipping Brandy. "Henry got nothing, no sex, until after we were married."

"I take it this was Henry's house?"

"It was his father's, until his father died."

"Do you have any family, Brenda.?"

"Two daughters, but they're both in their fifties now."

"What about Henry, is he still around?"

"No." Brenda filled her glass with more brandy. "He died a few years back."

"I'm sorry to hear it."

"He was almost fucking ninety, Tam."

"Then he lived to a fair age."

Brenda said that she thought so. "But how about you, what have you being doing?"

"Not as much as you, I don't think."

"Are you married?"

"No, I'm not married."

"Have you been married?"

I shook my head, no. "I'm a bachelor gay."

Brenda said she wouldn't have thought it. "But you can never tell these days, can you?" I let that go, because I wasn't really caring.

"I think you are still an attractive woman, Brenda."

"I think that you need glasses, Tam."

"You were always attractive to me," I said, "and you've

not changed, you're only older."

"Is that all, only older?"

I was feeling her leg up to her thigh, and she was attractive; a good full body and there are some women, some trick of nature, who can be attractive at any age. "You have still nice legs," I told her.

"It's a pity then that you are gay, isn't it?"

"I'm not really, it was only an expression."

She had had a few drinks, brandies by now; and something like the old Brenda, that she could not help but lead me on. "Are you up for it, Tam?"

Thank God for Viagra. I always carry some with me, and we had a wonderful few hours, before, too soon, I had to catch the coach and continue on my pilgrimage. Brenda ran back to my hotel where I was in time for breakfast. "At least now you know where I am if you are ever back in Cambridge". But we both knew we would not meet again. Our night had been as a trip though time, but it was not to be repeated. To try to repeat it would be madness, and the only thing was to let it go, which we did; and I have not heard from Brenda since.

It is a short trip from Canterbury to the Channel port of Dover, where we boarded the ferry to France; and, on the bus again, three hours or so to Lisieux, the home town of St Teresa. I had read her book, a memoir; and her simple faith is touching. Some fanaticism creeps into it, as, in a way, it must. Without fanaticism there would be no saints. They are of an extra-special mould, the saints, who, almost every single one of them, would have gladly died a martyr's death.

St Teresa was the youngest of five sisters, all of whom became nuns, so it is safe to say that religion was in the family. What praying in St Teresa's house when she was growing up? Not, I would hasten to add, that the praying in my house did me much good. I could shunt the blame on my environment, Father Gilmartin; who sickened me with his fee for my father's funeral mass, but the hard truth is that I was not religious. From fourteen years old my ambition was to become a heavyweight boxer, hopefully a champion. But it is totally wrong to compare myself; however loosely, with St Teresa and her gentle way, her time upon this earth.

We were, pilgrims all, taken to her house. As in one door and out the other, but suffice to say; for it was a large stone dwelling - leagues away from Bernadette's house or where the children of Fatima had once lived - that the family were well-doing, and becoming a nun was, in the material sense, something of a come-down. But five nuns in one family, and I was led to believe that the father; who was a watchmaker, had once thought to become a monk. However, rather than that he had met her mother, who, it was no surprise to me to learn, had almost become a nun herself. How they had gotten together I don't know, but the pious should give praise they did for from this union had come St Teresa.

I know people, quite a few, who have a great devotion to St Teresa, as well they might; for in all truth, she was a child of God as witnessed in her writing and by sister nuns who knew her.

It is harrowing reading, the death of St Teresa; a painful one, of tuberculosis, and I was close to tears when I finished it, for despite the pain, and she knew that she was dying, she retained her faith and love of God until the very end.

***

We were two days in Lisieux, with a side trip to Dunkirk. This was the first of the fighting beaches of the second world was and you can still see the bullet holes in the buildings in the town. The beach itself is wide and flat and lapping waves and it is hard to imagine a full army; or two armies, the British and the French, surrounded here by Hitler's tanks in September 1941. That they escaped, the sum of them; on every conceivable sort of craft short of a canoe, was lauded as the miracle of Dunkirk.

It is peaceful now, that beach of fury – there had been thousands dead and thousands more maimed and injured – and with so much human suffering I would hesitate on the miracle bit.

The following morning, we left Lisieux on the first leg of our journey home. The bus to Calais and the boat to Dover and back again to Canterbury, where we stayed the night, but I did not contact Brenda. It had crossed my mind to telephone her, but reason told me not to. She had a life of her own, as I had mine; and I was going with Rosie. I had been going with Rosie for a few years now, and I did not want to lose her. With Brenda, in a way, and for both of us, our surprise meet-up, it had been a complete one-off, and it would have been madness had I telephoned.

This time, in Canterbury; after our meal, and it was raining outside, I stayed in the hotel. Some conversation with fellow pilgrims before – Mary was speaking to some priest – I excused myself and retired early.

**

On my return from Morocco, I was far from well. A much weaker me than had been before. I had lost a lot of weight and whatever had happened to my system – that damn snake – I was not fit enough to work. This at a time when I needed to work, for, once again, I had no money and was staying with my mother. She did her best, my mother; if, thinking back, I was a case for hospital. But there had been many times when I should have been in hospital and had pulled through on my own, when I had been alone, with no-one to help. This time I had my mother, and little by little I began to mend, to regain my strength.

When, finally, I was fit enough I found employment in a steelwork. The job was shifts, something like the railway years before; but I was older now and lacked the verve I had back then, when, full of sap, I was reaching for a future. The bright lights. London. A whole new, swinging city; and I had thought that it would swing forever. In the sixties. I had no such illusions in the steelworks in the eighties. Far from it. What had been was done and gone and I was in my late thirties, and could not stop drinking; except, that was, when I had no money or was too ill to drink. This addiction, which had followed me up throughout my life, was becoming worse; much more severe the older I became. Hangovers were sore things now, and, as ever, the only cure was more drink. It had hit the point where I was scared to run out of drink and so carried a bottle of cheap wine with me to the steelwork.

This was a dangerous practice in a dangerous place, for accidents; some serious, were happening all the time. I remember one man who – he was standing next to me in a section they called the rolling mill – lost an eye to a spark of flying, red- hot steel. So it went, and I went too; out of the steelwork, after a fight with my immediate boss. An uncouth, brute of a man who liked to bully people. I was not for wearing it and the upshot was that I lost my job. It was no disaster, for I had hated the place and hated my boss, who, for the feeling was mutual, hated me. The only good thing, thinking back, was that both of us survived. This was pure luck, because we had tried our best to kill each other. Inside of a week or so I found another rotten, dead-end job; and after that another one, equally rotten, and so it went, job after job until, eventually, I was seen by a psychiatrist and ordered not to work at all.

***

In June of 1982 Pope John Paul 11 came to Glasgow. This was a huge event and there was an open-air mass in Bellahouston Park; which was about the only place big enough to accommodate the multitude, almost three hundred thousand people. I watched it all on television.

With my mother, who was astonished that such an event had come to pass; that the Pope of Rome should be saying a mass in Glasgow.

John Paul 11 was the most popular pope of modern times, not that I knew much, if anything about him. I had not been near a chapel for many years, and religion was not for me Despite this but I could not help but be impressed by John Paul 11. He had a benevolent look and an easy way and you sensed good will about him. This all added up to flesh and blood and an exceptional human being. He is now Saint John Paul, and that tells much about the man and how his fellow religious thought of him.

Back to Glasgow in June, 1983, where there was tremendous jubilation that the pope had come to Scotland. Amongst the Roman Catholics, that is. There was some muted, and not so muted, protest from the more die-hard protestants. For myself, I could not have cared less; this hullabaloo about the pope in Glasgow, and later that summer I would hear a surprising tale about him.

***

By now, out of work and registered as sick — and that was true, because I was very sick — I had become ill-natured. Distinctly hostile, mean and brooding, a touch of paranoia. This lent to difficulties, the usual fights and nights in jail and in and out of hospitals. It was no way to live; could you call it living, when at any time I might murder some-one or have some-one murder me. This was the hard fact of my existence when, and I had thought to be done with writing, I received a letter from a London film director who wanted to buy the rights to a story I had written years before.

The story, A NOBLE MOMENT had been published twice, in the Transatlantic Review and in a Faber anthology of new writers, introduction 6. The money on offer was far from vast, but enough; or so I thought, for me to start anew, a new life down in London.

To this end, and that the director would pay my travel costs, we arranged to meet in Euston Station. I was advised to his appearance, which was distinctive — he had a long black beard, for one thing — and I had a telephone number should, somehow, we miss each other.

I hoped we didn't, for I had no money. But skint or not I had a good drink in me when I boarded the train at Glasgow Central. I had no possessions, not even a watch; but and suddenly sprung, I was filled with hope that, somehow, this could be a turning point. A new life, for I was feed up with the jungle one I had been living

When the train reached London, I was far from sober. Where and how I got the booze I can't recall, for, as said, I had no money. But there had been countless times when I had had no money and yet had still acquired booze. A heroin addict might relate, the need of a fix; for it was as bad as that, my problem. I was to meet a man who might change my life yet, and for all my hope of a new and better life, I could not meet him sober.

The idea was I would be paid in cash. A cheque was no good to me because I did not have a back account. I was in need of a shave and a clean shirt, and; in all, in appearance, I was next door to a hobo.

My benefactor's first name was Martin, and he was with a friend and we, all three of us, adjourned to the lounge bar of a near-by pub where, before I signed the contract, I tried to bump-up the money for my story.

Martin was not for having it, and tried to explain it was budget thing and that he had no green light for filming the story. This turned out to be all too true, and so far, as I know; for I did not hear from him again, the story was not filmed.

In event, and I was desperate, we settled for the agreed sum and I soon found myself in possession of a hefty wad of banknotes. After that, the deal completed, Martin and his friend were not slow in leaving me, not that I can blame them. A writer. I was more like a drunken brickwork tramp. In the pub. I remember a long-nosed, quizzical-looking barman who had seen the money changing hands and he had to wonder what it was all about. I was not for telling him and, if I was drunk, I had been around and knew; an instinctive thing, that my safest bet was to leave that pub and keep the barman guessing.

I was feeling a bit on the lonely side and thought to buy some company. A prostitute, to be precise. With that in mind I began to make my way to Kings Cross when a sudden feeling of self-disgust stopped me in my tracks. Why this happened, and happened then; there, someplace between Euston and Kings Cross, is totally beyond me. I had been with prostitutes before and never, not once, before or after, the slightest twinge of self-disgust, so I can only think that, that night; whatever happened in my head, it was in the stars and that another; a most unusual fate awaited me.

***

I was something like myself again when, in the morning – for I had turned around and walked straight back to Euston – the train pulled into Glasgow. A sore head, but nothing more; and, certainly, nothing like the self-disgust I had felt in London. I put that down to the tramp I'd been and how the film guy and his friend had hurried to get away from me. That it had been more a question of self-esteem than self-disgust. But I did not know, not really; and so, chose to forget, and I was good at that, forgetting.

I must have been, for I had money enough to buy new clothes, but, as ever, I chose to drink. It was the easy way out. But out of what? It was all a conundrum, and the bald fact was that I did not like myself one bit. The man I was, had become. I had drinking acquaintances, but no real friends. How could I have had when I was anti-social? A man alone. The problem was I did not want to be a man alone, and I was fucking lonely.

Around this time, I went on a two-week bender that, once again, landed me in hospital. A head injury and a case of dehydration.

I was detained in hospital for three or four days and so had to sober up. But for how long? Once I was out, I would be back on the bottle. A mean, brooding drunkard. No wonder I had no friends, and even acquaintances in the lowest dives had begun to shun me, that I was a trouble maker. Fuck them, and their dives and I began to do my drinking in the house. And drinking wine, not spirits; because spirits were too hard on my stomach, especially now, when, in the mornings, I was drinking the best part of a bottle of wine to get me out of bed.

This was a bad, bad time in my life. But holding on, somehow. St Jude to the rescue once again? I did not, could not have cared what became of me. Some people hoped, so I have since been told, that I departed from this earth. A testament, if there was ever one, to my popularity.

A lone wolf, or I would think more accurately a dangerous hyena. For I was shunned by one and all, except that is for my dear mother. She was a gentle person and did not deserve a son like me. Anything other. One would think more a Cliff Richard or Daniel O'Donnell for a woman like my mother. A social person, unlike me; and she was well-liked, thought-off by everyone who knew her. Wee Mrs Healy. My mother was not five foot tall, and she had worked all her days; since the death of my father, as a school dinner lady and she was all of that, a lady; and I loved her and it breaks my heart that I was not the son that she deserved.

***

One of the days when I went out to buy my supply of booze, I bought a Glasgow Herald. Or The Herald, as it was now known. I forget the headlines, the news of the day; but – and I think it was fate, the whole thing; the sale of my story and the worthless feeling that had had me back from London – I chanced to read an advertisement, Doberman pups for sale. The ad went on to say that the pups were black and tan and of a good pedigree. Sitting, smoking; drinking wine, all of a sudden, I wanted a dog. It made no sense, but a lot of things in my life have made no sense. Not an ounce of it, and it was in my nature to be foolhardy; a man of action, and straight away, no pause for thought, I telephoned the advertiser. That same night I had a new wee pal, that; as proud as punch, was sitting in my lap. This whole thing, my drunken whim, would; in the years to come, prove to be a turning point.

Where, before, there had been only me, I had now a ward to care for, look after. I would, against all expectations; people who knew me or thought they knew me, provide my new wee mate with love and care and never, not once; not in all the years we were together, was an angry finger raised to him. We named the little pup – it was only five or six weeks old – after the film guy, Martin. Not that I had been too fond of him, but he had put up the money. This when, finally – Mary had thought to call him Tulip – we discovered that he was a boy. It must, easily, have taken six weeks for us to discover what sex Martin was and, when we did, that Tulip was too sissy a name for him. There was nothing sissy about Martin. He was a cocky wee creature from the very first. When I was there, that was. He was scared of nothing when I was there, but it was a different story if I went missing. He would howl like a wolf – I was supposed to howl back, from wherever I was? – and neither my mother or sister could do anything with him. Not a thing. He had fastened on to me and would not let go and as time went on this posed problems. There was no way Martin would have survived in a kennel, or; if he did, it would have wrecked his spirit, and I could not have that and, anyhow, I would have missed my pal too much.

This after a time, some months; because there had been a lot of feeling-out between myself and Martin. But I have been through all that, the Martin years in my book, *I have heard you Calling in The Night.* So enough, I think; that there was a reason – the work of St Jude, I would think - for my swift return from London. Had I not returned when I did, that very night when I got the money; there would have been no Martin and my life would have taken a different turn and the chances are that I would be dead by now, and a long time buried come to that.

As it was, we were together for ten years and in that time, I built a whole new – dare I use the word, loving? – relationship with my mother. I began to go to chapel with her and she came with us, Martin and me, on holiday. We would go to caravans and Mary sometimes joined us. A more stable me, with Martin; if, off and on, I would slip up and be as drunk as I had ever been. But there has to be downs along with the ups, and there were more ups than downs in the years that I had Martin, from 1983 to 1993. The good times. They would have a nightmare end, with Martin all but lame and my mother suffering a stroke. A bad one. It is well named, a stroke; for one moment you are okay and the very next an invalid. She had, my mother, gone out to a local shopping van, and; so, she told me later, had felt to be lifted high up, as over the roof-tops, before she collapsed and was carried back inside the house.

I thought she might die right then and there and – because I thought it was what she would want – I rushed to the chapel for the priest, Father O'Hagan, who administered the last rites over her. It is a frightful ritual, the last rites, and she was terrified and –I felt I like a man in chains, watching this –I wish now that I had done without the priest. When the doctor arrived, he phoned in an ambulance, and it was all so sudden – not unlike my father all those years before – and life changing and the house was not a home without her. Martin knew that something bad had happened as, all his life; since he was small, she had been there and was his pal and she would have nobody say a word against him.

My mother was in hospital for five months before I brought her home. This was against all medical advice, but where she was; in a geriatric ward that – because of falls – was full of bandaged heads and battered faces, I felt to have no option. This was after a particular visit when she had two black eyes and her nose was hurt and she looked to have been in a boxing ring. The problem was, as I soon discovered; visiting in a hospital is one thing and home nursing quite another. My mother was in a much worse, more fragile state than I had thought. All shrivelled up and paralyzed, with only the use of one hand. That was on the physical side, and the mental side was not much better. She had no short-term memory. None at all, and to try to cope with all of this the house had become a hospital, with a hospital bed and special sheets, for she was now incontinent. My poor mother. She had come to this. A commode and a wheelchair and a special chair, so that I could spoon her food. I had nurses in three times a day and

Mary helped, but there was only so much she could do. There was only so much I could do, and there were awful bouts of chest infections and, all in all, it could not last, nor could Martin; who, by now, was old and crippled, his back legs gone, but; and it was the only time I let him down, I could not bear to let him go

***

In the early summer of the following year – this after St Theresa in Lisieux –we went on pilgrimage to Poland, with, once again, Patrick and Father Hughie. We were to stay in a convent near Krakow, where a saintly nun; Sister Faustina, had once had a visitation from Jesus Himself, who had shown her his Sacred Heart.

Once again it was a taxi to Cardonald where we were re-united with a number of pilgrims who had been with us in Fatima, but there was no sign of Ralph; the guy who had told me his sad story – such a pathetic tale that it will hang in my head until I die - the last time around. When I enquired about him, I was told that he was sick, and that was even more sadness. He had, so it would seem, been out of luck since the very day he had been born. On the bus to Edinburgh Father Hugie told me that he would soon be going on a holiday to Kenya. "It is almost like returning home." One could only agree with that, all his years as a missionary; spreading the Good News, if I have often wondered what the Good News was, and is. Switch on a television and there is nothing but disasters, a whole catalogue of misery, of, in sum – for it is impossible to be specific – terrible misdoings. It is hard to speak of Good News in such a world, but the missionary manages to manage it. It beats me how, but he might be right and I am wrong for he has faith, that elusive thing that has always eluded me. We said the rosary on the bus, with; as added in, a prayer for a successful pilgrimage. At the airport Patrick was his usual, ebullient self – he had the gift to as radiate good will – and the flight left bang on time.

***

The original convent, where Sister Faustina was once a nun, has been expanded and there is a substantial sub-building with several floors and lots of modern, en-suite rooms. The restaurant is on ground level and you could see the street and a little corner shop from it. The shop was an almost spitting image of the old shops in the Gorbals and when I mentioned this to Mary I asked if she thought we could steal some spam from it?

"Mary said she thought not.

"We can't run that fast anymore."

"But it was fun at the time, wasn't it?"

"Until you were nearly caught it was — remember that guy who chased you?"

"I'll never forget that guy who chased me.

The food was plain but wholesome and plenty of it. The major fault was that the place was far too crowded, chairs back-to-back; and I thought the meal times should be staged to accommodate the — for there had to be another four, or even five — various groups of pilgrims. Mary was of the same opinion, but; much like me, thought it better not to say, too, as it were, rock the boat of a pilgrimage just begun.

After our meal we went out from the complex, on to the streets and roads of Poland. It was late May and the

night was cool and good for walking and we walked all the
way to Krakow. Four miles or six? I don't know. We were
in no hurry. Not then. To begin. In the early evening. But
sitting outside a cafe in Krakow – it is old and quaint, all
cobblestone streets and soaring spires – when I looked at a
clock, I was surprised to discover that it was almost
midnight. Convents and monasteries; places of prayer, are
notorious for locking-up early.

Ten o'clock is late for them. We, for whatever reason,
that we were in a quaint strange place, had mis-judged the
time and it was no surprise when we got back – in a taxi –
that the convent was in darkness. There was a big, wooden,
shield-shaped door and I pressed the bell and pressed
again. No answer. What to do? There was now a chill in the
air and I kicked the door and, eventually, it was opened by
an old, thin, bent man – he was in his nightshirt - who had
to be a hundred. We knew the way to our rooms, which
was just as well, for; going by the look of him, he was not
amused. Mary thought we had woken him up.

"He was far from pleased," I can tell you that. "

"It won't happen again."

"You bet it won't." We were in the corridor outside her room. "He reminded me of Methuselah."

I agreed. "He's far from young."

"I think he's a priest."

"You do?"

"Well, he's not the night watchman, is he?"

"No," I said, "but he's probably back sleeping again."

"Do you think?"

"I hope he is."

Mary said so did she, and that was it, our first night in Poland.

***

Breakfast was a self-service affair and then it was off to a mass said by Father Hughie. Following that we had a tour round the convent, with the highlight being Sister Faustina's former cell. A small, spartan place where she had lived and prayed and practiced self-flagellation. The lash she had used was still in view, and I can only surmise; as she saw it, some sort of cleansing, purification. Sister Faustina was far from the first practitioner of this ritual, and it is safe to say that she won't be the last. Far from it.

Some need in the pious. I can see no sense at all in it, but, again, I can see no sense in my devotion to St Jude. Yet when I am down, I pray to him and afterwards I feel a lift. Sister Faustina must have had felt much more than that, a lift; when the Lord Himself appeared to her and a vision of His Sacred Heart. It was radiant with shafts of multi-coloured light and, by way of an artist who re-produced what she had seen, it has since become an icon in the Roman Catholic Church. There are copies of it in almost every chapel in the world, and especially in Poland. Sister Faustina died of tuberculosis in 1938 at the age of33years.

***

One of the days on our pilgrimage to Poland we were taken on a trip to Wadowice, the town where Pope John Paul II had been born and raised. It has hardly changed in at all since then, and we had a mass in the chapel where he had served as an altar boy.

A man of the people, was John Paul II. His visit to Glasgow, which I have tried to describe, was evidence of that. No king or queen could have been made more welcome, not by the Catholics, anyhow. We had a follow-up in 2010 by Pope Benedict, who, too, said an open-air mass in Bellahouston Park. This again was televised and a huge congregation, but; somehow, it missed the magic, the sheer exuberance of John Paul's visit. Benedict, it appeared to me, had all the warmth of a plaster cast and could not compare with John Paul II. A hands-on saint – he was canonised by Pope Francis in 2014 – who, glamour-wise, was next door to a film star.

John Paul's father was a doctor, an affluent one, so there was no material poverty in the life of the young Karol Wojtyla, as John Paul was known then. But his mother had died when he was nine, so he was denied a lot on the emotional side. Life could have been no bed of roses for the future pope, if, in his later life he hid it well, as was becoming of the man. There might have been an awful lot John Paul hid well. The war years. Poland was in the thick of things, occupied by both Germany and Russia and, at the time he came to Glasgow, I knew a Polish man who swore that he had served with him in the German army.

"You jest."

"I do not."

What to say? This man was far from a fool and not given to lying, or, more precisely, to telling lies that were not to his advantage, and it was no big deal, not to him, that his old army mate had become the pope.

"They were crazy times back then, and lots of Polish guys joined the German Army."

When I said I thought he was mistaken, that he had the wrong man, I was informed that Karol (the pope, as he had supposedly been known in the army) had served as a motor bike despatch rider on the first push of the German advance into Russia.

"He was always smiling, and was a damn good soldier."

He was?

"I don't think you believe me."

"I don't know what to think. Sometimes men can look alike, and it is a long time ago."

The Polish guy said that it was like yesterday to him, and re-assured me that the soldier and the pope were the same man. "He was always smiling and we used to call him smiler."

I dismissed the story for a mistaken identification, the pope as soldier in Hitler's army, but agreed with him that, all in all, it did not matter, if, I have to say, if it was true, that stranger things have happened.

***

On another day trip we were taken to Auschwitz. It is a vast, a sprawl of a place and, even on the approach to it, a feeling of gloom, of inhumanity. The tortured souls who went up in smoke. Some of the original huts still stand and there are streets of sorts; but what happened here – as a hell on earth- proved to be too much for me and I did not hang around, and the same could be said for Mary. We went back to our bus - it was one of many, because the horror that was Auschwitz has become a tourist attraction, if it beats me why – where we waited for our fellow pilgrims to return. For myself, I wished that I had never come to this dreadful place; as a sense of evil in the air, and, really, it is no place for a pilgrim. It is no place for any one of any sensitivity and it is my firm believe it should be bulldozed down and the grass should then grow over it.

***

My mother was at home for the best part of a year, but an unequal, uphill struggle that could not last, go on; and finally, at my doctor's urging – that my own health was suffering – I agreed on a respite of two weeks. I had taken her out of hospital but I could not take her back, and I almost cried the day she left; in an ambulance in her wheelchair.

With my mother back in hospital I did what I had to do for Martin. There was no option, no other way out; and no other dog to take his place, not then nor now, and I still miss him. I miss my mother even more, but; with her, I had not to do what I had with him, as act as an executioner. It was how I felt on that winter night – it was late November and dreich and cold and I remember a first lighted Christmas tree – when I carried him out of the house and into a waiting taxi. The vet was a thin man with a black moustache and he knew that I was coming. There was no words spoken and I held Martin – he was on his feet, his own four paws – while the vet bent down and felt for a vein and seconds later, four at most, Martin fell down on his chest, bumping it against the floor.

***

I got drunk that night and was drunk for days, but; with my mother back in hospital, I had to sober up to bring her home again. Some hope. While she was still in hospital my mother suffered yet another chest infection that all but finished her. At this time, just off of booze and the sweats and shakes and all the rest, I had a one-night stand with a lady doctor, who, I think, had taken pity on me. I can come up with nothing else, and never; not in all my life, had I needed some-one as I needed her that night, too, in a way, as ward away my demons. She was younger than me, and there was no question; as she made clear, of anything ongoing. But I remember that night and her and how I was; as full of dread and that death would be a mercy, with a lasting, thankful, clarity.

After a week or so my mother regained her consciousness. But the chest infection had taken a toll and it was now out of the question for me to take her home. It was now December and the festive season, Christmas and New Year. What a pain in the arse, the whole thing; jingle bells and fucking snowmen and on New Year's Eve, to pass the time, I watched television. A Scottish channel. They used to make a big thing of New Year in Scotland. The Highland Fling. Men in kilts and bonnie lassies. Out with the Old and in with the New. I wished it was that simple, that one night could make a difference; and I was all alone and missing Martin and no bonnie lassie, none at all, could have cheered me up that night.

***

January is a long, cold; usually rainy month in Scotland. In the Victoria geriatric ward, my mother was on the top floor, where they housed the worse of cases. She had recovered from the chest infection and was sitting in a chair beside her bed when I went to visit her, and I visited every day and sometimes twice a day. Mary did too, if, somehow, rather than draw us closer, as companions in adversity, it was pulling us apart. Half of the time we were hardly even on speaking terms. Chronic illness can do strange things, if I would doubt our mother knew — this rift, what it was, between her children. As time went on, we made it up and became great pals, and there is nothing I would not do to help my sister.

One of the days when she was at home my mother had said. "I don't want tae leave youse."

It had broken my heart when she said that. A moment of lucidity. She did not want to leave us, but, as she must have known, the world was not for keeping her. An odd thing, my mother did not mention Martin; and, if I did not say, I think she knew that he was dead. But I will never know, not for sure — you have one person before a stroke and another person after it — but I chose to think she knew okay, Thomas's wee dog.

January went to February, when she suffered another stroke. This one took away her speech, but it did not seem to bother her, as, perhaps, she was now immune to suffering. A total loss of dignity, as helpless as a baby. Yet still, for all of that, she would smile to me and appear to listen when I spoke, and I had never been as proud of her as I was in those last days.

***

Galloway is in the Scottish Uplands, not far from the English border. The House of Prayer, where I was going, is hosted by Peter and Suzie Seed. They own a large farm, and Suzie is a convert. I have often noticed on my travels; on pilgrimage, that converts make the best Catholics. Why, for what reason, I do not know, but it is a fact. Suzie is a great example. An intelligent, highly capable woman she runs her retreats with tremendous passion.

Suzie and Mary were very friendly, and a big hug on our arrival. With Father Hughie who would give the retreat and who had driven us there, from his parish in Cardonald, where else? For accommodation we had small clean rooms in a sort of dormitory called a bothy. This is an old Scottish word for dwelling place. There were some sixteen guests, mostly women, who, all of them, were into prayer. What else? A weekend of it. On the first night, after a meal, we had a service. Father Hughie in good voice and, listening to him, I knew the retreat would be successful.

After the service, much as we had in Poland on our first night there, Mary and I went out for a walk. There was no chance this time of returning late and being locked out. It was a glorious night at the end of June when it is rarely dark in Scotland. A sort of gloaming all night long. There was a path from the farm that led to a brook and you could hear it gurgle, but that was all; the only sound, as, all over the land, in the rolling fields of Galloway, a huge hush and I said to Mary that I was taking a vow of silence.

"Are you joking?"

"I am not."

"For how long?"

"Until I say goodbye to Peter and Suzie."

"Why, what for this vow of silence?"

"I don't know what for." I had taken such a vow before, in a monastery in Morey; in the far North of Scotland, and had, when I was allowed to speak again, felt the better for it. "I just feel like peace and quiet."

"It's a bit strange, but it's up to you – when do you intend to begin this vow of silence?"

I said nothing.

"Have you already begun?"

I put a finger to my lips.

"This is crazy," Mary said. "Are you not supposed to warn people that you will be taking a vow of silence?"

But I could not say, reply to her. This sudden, unexpected vow, for; two minutes before, it had been the last thing on my mind.

Walking back to the farm house. In silence. It went with the night, somehow; the quiet of the country-side, if, I thought – for I can be amusing, sometimes – that Mary was disappointed. A walking statue by her side, and it would remain that way until the retreat was ended.

***

The day began with morning prayer and following that was breakfast. It was served on a long, straight, wooden table that could accommodate the entire company of retreatants. Father Hughie his usual, sociable self; but he must have heard about my vow for not a word to me. In

Galloway, where I began to go long walks, as, once, years before, I had gone long walks with Martin. In the country, when he was young; all lithe and quick and full of fun, high spirits. He was scared of nothing, or only me; if I got drunk and, in a way, let us both down. Out time together, and it was only time that did for us. An ageing Martin. He was eight and a half years old when my mother had first suffered her stroke and, in the time since then, it was touch and go for who went first, Martin or my mother.

I should have been married, a father; grandfather, when my mother had her stroke. It is the usual way of things but I was never usual. An oddity, if I am honest, for, for all the women in my life I never, or only once; my affair with the head teacher, thought to marry. It had rebounded on me then, when my mother took her stroke. A too-old me and my too-old dog. But I came through. Somehow. It is an odd fact that oddities often do. Buck the odds, when more normal men might flounder.

It was, despite my vow or because of it, a good weekend in Galloway. Father Hughie. I attended all the services and, that good man, I felt the benefit of them. Why? Could it be that I was searching; hoping that, in such pious company, something might rub off?

***

My mother died in 1994 I had been expecting her death, but it was still a shock when it finally came. She had been in a coma and I was barely back from the hospital when the telephone rang and the person on the end told me that I should hurry back because the end was very near. As if I had not known that, and I would suspect; as I suspected then, that my mother was already dead. The telephone call was at eight in the morning and when, less than thirty minutes later, I arrived at the hospital I was told I was too late. I was offered the usual condolences, and after all her suffering I could only hope, wherever she was, it was a much better place than the place she had departed from, but; dear God, I was missing her already.

***

I did not view my mother's corpse, I was too put out and it would have done no good and I did not want to see her dead. Then, alone in the house, some hours later; just before mid-day, I heard my mother speak.

"Oh, hello John."

This in a joyous voice of a woman in her prime and it took me way back, to the days of my earliest childhood.

There was nothing more, only that; those three words, but wherever she was, in whatever void, I knew she had connected with my father, whose name was John.

Ever since then, that experience; so totally unexpected, I have believed in a spirit world, and, after death, wonderful new adventures.

***

I continued to drink after my mother had passed away, or over. But I was becoming older and, should I get into a fight; as I sometimes did, I was now little more than a punching bag. I took some beating when I was in my early fifties. Real brutal stuff. But that is neither here nor there, not now; and it did not stop me drinking. And I had no intention to stop drinking. I was a single man and could do as I chose, and if I chose to drink then I would drink.

During the home nursing I had been drunk just once; a two-day binge, during which the nurses had threatened to go on strike.

But that time was over, done; and I was back again, and worse than ever, on the alcoholic way. This would go on for the next few years, until, one unforgettable day, I was too drunk to get out of bed, to make it to the toilet, and I pissed myself. This was in the early afternoon, but I was still wearing my trousers from the night before; and the warm flow of urine soaking them and me and, still, for all of that, I could not get out of bed.

They say in Alcoholics Anonymous that; no matter what has happened in the past, there is always a new first for any alcoholic, and this was a first for me. I had never peed a bed before. It was a September day and I had the window curtains open and bright sunshine lighting up the room. Where I lay as trapped, as caught in a sunbeam, drenched in sweat and urine. I had lain on streets, battered stupid; covered in blood, but it had been not half as bad as this. My humiliation. Some hours passed, then another flood. Hot urine. I can only say that I was more than mortified. You have to hit rock bottom at the drinking game before you quit, and this was mine. I knew it then, in my bed; and it was night by now and the room in darkness.

Sometime around three in the morning I arose and managed to strip off my soiled clothing. I felt like a smoke but my hands shook so badly that I could not hold a cigarette. When I sat in my chair, I was shocked by the cold of a bottle of wine I could not remember buying. There were other bottles and cans on the floor that, too, were news to me, that I could not remember buying. Some three of wine and cans of beer, of super lager. It was impossible to hold a glass and I drank the wine straight from the bottle. A hearty draught, to say the least. About half of the bottle. I felt the heat of it inside my gut and never, not ever, did I welcome a drink more than I did that morning.

After a little I was able to roll a smoke and fill a glass. I was wearing a vest, but that was all. Barefoot in the house, in the dark of the early morning. I opened a can of the super lager and drank it slowly. An amber brew that had a kick. By now, my drinking, a can of normal beer was next to worthless. I could remember nothing of the past few days or going to bed or coming home. Wherever I had been, it was not to a barber's anyhow; not going by my beard. A good week's growth, and I was filthy and could not shower. Had I tried to shower I would have fallen, so I had to just put up with it. Me. My reek of sweat and urine. Still, I was beginning to feel much better. A bit like human. That and, somehow, something in the root of me, I knew that this would be my last hangover

Peeing the bed had been the straw that broke me. I won't try to puzzle why it broke me, for over the years I had been in much worse, more serious trouble; but that was the one I could not take, and I knew it then; that night or morning. After a few more drinks I went back to bed, and for all it was wet; sodden in urine, I fell fast asleep.

When I awoke again, I had a few more drinks and felt fit to shower, to have a shave. A change of clothing. But I was soon shaking again and, as is the way, in sore need of more drink to steady up again.

This is not an advisable way to stop drinking, but there was drink available and I was far from superman. More, in all; during this last drink, a mouse of a man and how to turn my life around?

I tried to read, but had no concentration. Once again it

was dark outside and I put the television on. The ten o'clock evening news. I did not know what day it was and was not really caring. My stupendous bender. I was lucky to be alive, in, outwith some bruising and a missing tooth, the one piece. Not that I felt all that lucky to be alive, the struggle I was sure to face. I was loath to be sober for the rest of my life but, loath or not, I knew I must. Be sober. It had, and all because of my peeing the bed, become; for all I was still drinking, the most important thing in the world to me.

I felt to go out, to get some air, but; for I felt weak, there was a danger I might collapse. So, I stayed in the house, but; as chance would have it, I had a visit from a man named Davie, who was something of a pal of Mary's.

This guy had been though the mill himself, drink-wise. He had lost a lot, his wife and children; but had been sober for the past six years. I had first met with Davie some time back, in Alcoholics Anonymous. The program there had worked for him, and he lived near-by and would visit sometimes, usually after meetings. This particular night I was more than glad to see him. A non-judgmental sort of man. It happened that, at the time, Davie was having a bit of woman trouble, and we spoke about that, and not about my drinking.

He stayed for a couple of hours, and I liked the guy and felt the better for his visit. It had broken the night, and if he could do it; stop the drinking, so could I. Not that I said anything to him about stopping drinking. He would have not believed me if I had, and there was no way I was for telling him about my peeing the bed.

By some weird coincidence a couple of days later Mary told me that the Pioneers were holding a meeting the coming Sunday in a local chapel hall.

"Who are the Pioneers?"

"People who don't drink."

"Do you think they can help me stop drinking?"

"I think they are worth a try."

Davie was there and he agreed. "Anything is worth a try."

"It is a society of total abstinence," Mary told him.

Davie said that was fine with him and we arranged to meet the following Sunday when, without much ado – that it was no big thing – we all took an oath to refrain from drink and none of us has drank again.

***

Children can ask good questions, and; as I read someplace, Pope Francis was hit by two of them, from ten or eleven year olds. The first question concerned what God did and where He was before he created the world? Pope Francis would have come up with something, hopefully; but I am not too sure his explanation would have – what after all is a mystery –made much sense The second question was why, if God wanted us in the Kingdom with Him, then why did we not go straight there?

That, that The Lord works in mysterious ways would, I'm sure, have been the answer. Why not, for it covers the lot; and if the Passion of Christ was preordained, then so too was the role of Judas. One could argue that it was not his fault to do what he did when, after all, some-one had to play the part and rather than scorn he deserves a bit of sympathy.

***

Dublin, 2008. It was the coldest October for fifty years. An icy grip that reminded me of Glasgow in the fifties. When you had went to school you were all wrapped up in caps and scarves and I remember slides that went on and on for, almost, the full length of a street. I can't think of a slide in recent times, because, simply, it is not cold enough to have the ice. Back then it was plenty cold and you had icicles, and some of them long; like five or six feet, hanging down from the tenement roofs, that, should one of them snap, would fall down and kill you. Not that I recall anyone who was ever killed by an icicle in Glasgow.

I saw now icicles or slides in Dublin, more, because it had not rained, a hard dry chill that chaffed your lips and stung your nose.

It was the 27th of the month and we had taken the airport bus into the centre of this cold city with the intention of another bus to take us to a place named Moone, where we were booked into a small monastery named Bolton. We would be back in Dublin on the 28th for a visit Whitefriars Street Church where they have a shrine to St Jude.

"You don't think we should find a hotel and stay the night here, in Dublin?" Mary said no.

"They will be expecting us in Bolton, and we are to stay there for three nights."

So, we boarded a bus for Moone. Wherever that, Moone might be. I had never heard of it, but had gone along when Mary had made the booking. This cold place. It was forty or more years since I had been in Dublin, and the city had changed completely. I would doubt to have known a city that had changed as much as Dublin. It used to be all priests and nuns and Irish men and women. No more. Half of the population seemed to be of foreign extraction and nary a priest or nun in sight. It detracted a lot from its character, but that was the price to pay for economics. The European Union. A booming Ireland. Gone were the days of women in rags and their children in bare feet. There was no-one wanted a return to that, those times; but this new Dublin – it was awash with drugs, so I had heard – was hardly even Irish.

On the bus on our way to Moone in, as it turned out, the County of Kildare. Our driver was a black man and I thought the cold must be worse for him than it was for us. Mary voiced that this was nonsense. "He was probably born here in Ireland."

"That makes a difference?"

"It makes all the difference, and he's got plenty of fat by the looks of him."

And he had, that and a jolly roly-poly look; steering his bus out of Dublin on the road to Kildare

Moone is a small, rural village which I thought was unremarkable. Or remarkable only for the cold, that is. It was dark when we reached it and a high star-filled sky and we asked a shopkeeper; a dour-faced man to phone a taxi for us.

"To where are you going?"

"Bolton Abbey."

"I'll drive you there for five Euros."

It was a good enough deal, and we reached the Abbey in about ten minutes. A foreboding looking, gloomy, place that was at the end of a gravelled driveway.

"It looks more like a haunted house that a monastery," I

remarked to Mary. She said she didn't care and to ring the doorbell.

"I'm freezing, standing out here." The door was opened by a burly monk who introduced himself as Brother Bernard, and,

"You are our guests from Scotland?"

I said we were, and; as in from the cold, Brother Bernard led us through to the dining room where the evening meal was just being served.

"You will be ready for something to eat," he said.

There were three other guests, all women. The cold weather opened the conversation. None of the women had known such cold, and one complained that the heating was switched off at nine o'clock. "It's not good enough."

"Have you spoken to Brother Bernard?"

"I have, but it's the abbot's decision and he won't relent."

Mary enquired about the bus times back to Dublin, for she wanted to be in Whitefriars Street Chapel for St Jude's day the following morning.

The woman said not to worry because she was leaving the monastery the following morning and her son was coming to pick her up and, as she stayed in Dublin, it would be no problem for him to run us there. "Sure, and it's the least that I can do to help two Scottish pilgrims.

My room had a single bed and a table and chair and a huge crucifix and, most importantly, a radiator. So, it was warm enough, to begin; when I went to bed, but I was awakened in the early hours by a deathly chill. A real freeze. The room as an ice box. I looked around for more blankets, but there were none, so I covered myself over with my coat. The heating went back on at six o'clock, when, how I saw things, the mean abbot; it should have been on all though the night.

After breakfast the son appeared and, it was still half dark at nine o'clock, we were driven into Dublin. I sat in the front with him and he told me that it had been on the news that it was now the coldest October in living memory. I did not doubt that. The fields of Ireland white with frost that shimmered under a low, red, angry-looking sun. I asked him if there were no reported cases of frost-bite? There had indeed. A tramp had been found dead in a park, frozen solid." From the back of the car his mother said,

"God have mercy on his soul."

"Mary said, "Amen to that."

The son said he was not a religious man, but that no person should freeze to death in modern-day Ireland."

I told him that many a tramp had been frozen to death in modern-day Scotland.

On we went. On the way to Dublin. The mother said she would be glad to get home.

"I'll make meself a nice wee cup of tea and have a nice wee buttered scone."

Mary asked the son in he knew the Carmelite chapel in Whitefriars Street, where we were going.

"It has a shrine to St Jude."

He said he did not know about the shrine but that he knew the chapel and would take us there. "It's not far away from where we're going."

The woman said her son knew Dublin like the back of his hand. "He is a taxi driver."

"It has changed a lot, Dublin," I said, "since the last time I was there."

"When was that?"

"About forty something years ago – it was full of priests and nuns from what I recall."

The son said he was only thirty-six years old, but had heard about the old days. "It was a different city then, so they say."

"A better one," his mother said. "We might have been poor, but we had our faith and Dublin was still Irish."

"It's full of immigrants now," I said, "going from what I've seen."

"That's what I mean, that it's not Irish any more – or even catholic, come to that."

"You get nothing for nothing, and immigrants are part of the European Union." The son was a smoker and a cigarette dangled from his mouth. "There are no borders, so what can you expect?" I told him it was the same in Glasgow. "We have a huge mosque on the south side. They call it the Islamic Centre." The mother was strangely understanding about the muslins and their mosques. "In the old days when the Irish went to other lands, they took their priests and chapels with them and the Muslims are just doing the same."

It was hard to disagree with that, and the son dropped us off in Whitefriars Street, right beside the chapel. A freezing Dublin. I was beginning to think this must be the coldest October ever in Ireland. The chapel was big and it had many shines but not too many radiators. A definite chill inside the place. Row after row of wooden pews and Blessed Titus Bransma, whoever he was — it was the first I had encountered Blessed Titus — and another new one, St Albert of Sicily, to name but two of the shrines in there. There had to be six or seven, and St Jude. He was dressed as ever in his biblical clothes with his little axe or hatchet.

I once saw a statue of St Jude where he was carrying a hammer, which was a mistake I am sure of the artist — that or he had just wanted to be different. I said my usual hello to him and Mary, for her part, spent a good while in prayer. When she finally finished, we discovered the chapel had a hall next door that was well-heated and sold fast food and we treated ourselves to sausage rolls. Mary said it was good of the woman and her son to have run us into Dublin. "It was a bit of luck, meeting her."

"It certainly was."

"But now we need to go back again."

"I'll ask in here if they can phone a taxi to take us to the bus station."

Mary agreed. "It's too cold to hang about in Dublin."

When the taxi came it was driven by a Pole from Krakow, where; given this chronology, we had yet to visit. It was a short run and we caught the bus with nothing to spare, as it was pulling out of the station.

"Thank God for this," Mary said, "or St Jude, for getting us out of Dublin."

I was inclined to agree, for; had we missed the bus, it was a two hour wait for the next one.

This time the driver was Irish, a man from Wexford; where, via lots of other places, the bus terminated. He was a talkative type and when he asked why we were going to Moone Mary explained that we were Catholics on a pilgrimage and were staying in Bolton Abbey. The driver said he had heard of it, but that was all. "I've never been in a monastery."

"But you are a Catholic?"

"I am," he said, "but it's a wee while since I attended me duties."

Attended his duties. It had been years since I had heard that one. But at least he was Irish, born and bred, so he said. On his bus, where; eventually, we found seats and had just settled down when a woman in front turned around and asked if we knew about the murders in Moone? "There's been five or six of them," she said, "all young women."

"Five or six?

"So, it seems."

"I haven't heard of any murders, and that's a lot of murders."

She was round faced with bright white hair and blue eyes and a stubby nose and very, very Irish looking. "There might be more, for a lot of lassies have gone missing."

"Lassies don't just go missing."

"In Moone they do."

"Has there been arrests?"

"Not so far."

"Then the murderer's still loose?"

"There might be more than one murderer." The woman's voice took on a low, confidential tone. "Have you heard of devil worship?"

"I have, but I would hardly think of devil worship in rural Ireland."

"Then you don't know the half of it."

"I'm not too sure that I want to know the half of it."

"There's a lot of witches here in Ireland, so there is."

"Witches are not murderers."

The woman said she was not so sure. "I've heard rumours about black masses where they require a human sacrifice."

I thought that she was round the twist. "Then the police should put a stop to it."

"The witches don't just stand up and declare themselves, and they say there's important people in the covens."

"They do?"

"Aye," she said, "there's been whispers about the clergy, and even the police themselves."

"Then you think it's a sort of conspiracy?"

"I don't know what to think, but lassies are dead and there's no-one been arrested."

Mary said it was news to her; these murders here in Moone, and she wondered why, all of this; if lassies had been murdered, it had escaped the attention of the media. "It's as bad or worse than the Boston Strangler." The woman said it was all of that, and she could only hope the murders at Moone would soon be in the news "Big time," she said. "All those poor young lassies." I thought the witches and devil worship a bit much, but; certainly, when I enquired at the monastery, I discovered the story was true – young women murdered and others missing, that, to the outside world, for whatever reason, had been covered-up, a whitewash job that I found astonishing.

***

Moone is a small monastery. I would think some seven

or eight monks and a couple of brothers along with Brother Bernard, who was the guest master. It was not an easy life for Brother Bernard, who was in his eighties but fit and strong, as; in his brown cassock, a warrior monk of old. He had huge, calloused hands and one thing for sure he did not shirk his duties. At breakfast time, just after mass, he would be out in the open with his face wrapped up against the cold – and it was very, very cold – armed with a spade or pitchfork, to toil in the grounds.

I liked the brother, how he was. A manly man with a humorous, easy way. Which was just as well, because some of his guests were quite unusual.

There were six of us, including a nun and a man who claimed to be a former monk, but was now married. This guy claimed, when he was a monk, to have been lifted up on the rope while ringing the church bell – his fellow monk on the other rope had been nicknamed Tarzan and was noted for his strength –and to have been locked in the belfry for three days. He had never recovered from this ordeal, and it had wrecked his hearing.

I did not believe this story, and neither did the nun or Mary; and we had severe doubts if he had ever been a monk at all.

Still, I have to say he was amusing; to me, if not to Mary or the nun, who, to put it bluntly, thought him screwy.

His wife – they had supposedly married in his former monastery, where all his old fellow monks had cheered him loudly – was a thin, stringy-looking woman who, and he was the first to tell you, was not the full shilling. Another odd guest was a thin hunchbacked man who spoke not a word to anyone, except, that was, for Brother Bernard, who had known him for years and who told us not to bother him. "He likes to be alone."

In every monastery, in the evening; you have vespers and compline when all the monks assemble and sing and pray on the altar of the chapel. Both of the services have a certain charm, as, in a way, all chanting Latin, they are out of time, as in another century. This appealed to me and I was a fond attender if, the chanting monks; their ancient prayers, pleas or what, I was lost in the translation. Words of wisdom, I don't know; but they were certainly much repeated. Night after night and all over the world, in every Catholic monastery, a perpetual chant that, it is safe to say, will go on and on until the end of time. This, the evenings in the chapel; in a half-dark with, on the altar, burning candles and wafting incense, was what I enjoyed most about Bolton Abbey. That and the sky outside, which, in the frozen nights, was clear and bright that I might observe the heavens.

Ever since my childhood I have had an interest in astronomy, the night sky. This had been blunted by my drinking, but shortly after I sobered up, I acquired (and carried with me everywhere) powerful binoculars the better to enjoy my study, and I was thrilled by the view I had in Ireland. In a field outside the abbey. It was really freezing and thick hoar frost and I wished that I had warmer clothing – as a balaclava and a pair of gloves, that I might view for longer. The universe. It is a fantastic jigsaw that will never be gleaned, much less than understood. You might chart some stars, but there are other, further ones and further ones again. A never-ending multitude that reach out to infinity, whatever that, infinity, might be. Who knows? Not me. But I do know that, in the perfect set of the universe, man has the wisdom of a flea, and one of the nights, in the field, when I was viewing through my binoculars, I felt suddenly dizzy and more than mortal and that nothing was right and everything wrong and, as all of a sudden, what I had been taught at school when I was six years old came back to me. *God was, is, and ever will be.*

***

One of the monks ran us to Moone on the morning of our departure. A seven o'clock bus to Dublin airport. It was still dark and the moon and stars and our frosted breaths, waiting for the bus. On the street. There were four or five people waiting with us. This place of murders, of young females going missing. It was a thought to ponder, standing there; what, in this world, the human animal – and I use that word advisably – can stoop to.

The bus, when it came, was full of workers, mostly Irish; if, here and there, the inevitable emigrant. The Emerald Isle. The emigrant could be well excused if they thought to have made a mistake and that they were now in Iceland. There were a few stops, collecting people, before we were in Dublin, where the whole bus emptied and it was only us; Mary and me, still on board when it reached the airport.

It is an hour's flight, Dublin to Glasgow, and with no customs; baggage checks, we were back in Mary's house before mid-day.

"I bet you're glad to be home," she said, "for a bit of heat if nothing else."

"I suppose I am, but I loved the evening services – you know, vespers and compline."

"I thought you might."

"I did, and I will miss them tonight – I can tell you that right now."

Mary said that so would she. "I liked the peace and quiet."

***

I have understated the drinking business. It was far from easy stopping it, and I was far from well at that first meeting of the pioneers. Indeed, for all my resolve; my peeing the bed, I was none too sure if I could or would abstain. A life of total abstinence. I knew it was the only answer, but tell that to a drinking man; and I was only days away from my last drink. I have often wondered, had I been alone; for I was feeling dreadful, if I would have sneaked into a pub. God knows, and I had finished what booze I had in the house and; this sudden withdrawal, the following day I phoned in the doctor. It was not the first time I had to phone in the doctor, so it was no surprise to him to find me in such a way.

I told him I was finished with drinking, and, "I mean it this time." He told me that it was about time.

"It's killing you — do you know that?"

"I've known it for years, but I still continued drinking."

"Then what's so different this time?"

"I've had enough."

"Will you still think you've had enough this time next week or next month?"

"I hope I will."

My doctor was an Indian and, I have to say, a more than understanding man. "I could call in AA for you."

"I've already tried AA and it didn't work."

"But it might this time."

I told the doctor no, that I was not in the mood for talking. "I don't feel too good."

"I don't doubt that."

"You can see me shaking."

The doctor shook his head in a sad way. "You should think before you drink," he said, "because it will always come to this. It is something in your make-up." I thought it was more long practice, but could not be bothered arguing and so I agreed with his assessment.

After this, our little conversation, he wrote out a prescription for Librium. It was a massive dose I was prescribed and I was full of it, Librium, for the next few days. But half drugged or not I was still awfully nervy. A good drink would have straightened me out, and I knew that and I was sorely tempted. A bit of ease to my troubled mind. It had happened before, and often; another drink to forget the last one. It would have been the easiest thing to have broken my oath, but, too, there was the nag in my head that this was a final chance.

Back to that Sunday, the pioneers; with Mary and Davie

and, after our pledges, walking back to Mary's house. A cup of coffee. I felt more like a bottle of wine, and it is very easy to forget. I knew it all, the self-deceit, and yet I was still tempted. A small drink. The pioneers met once a month, and they would never know. A cheating member, but cheating who?

Davie had sobered up in rehab. A six week stay. It was his second time there, in a retreat that worked on AA principals.

"I hated the place, but it has worked this time; until now that is."

"Six years," I said.

"A day at a time," Davie said. "You can only live a day at a time."

"Then I will need to take my pledge that way."

"It is the only way."

Mary asked: "Do you think you'll make it?"

"I hope I do."

Davie offered to accompany me to AA meeting. "It will get you out of the house if nothing else." I said I would think about it, but; my life-time pledge, it hardly seemed like a day at a time for me.

"There's lots of good guys in AA."

And so, there were, still are; but I was not in the mood for company. My missing front tooth and a looming depression. It is always the same when you come off of a bender, nerves and depression that, half of the time, you just feel like hiding.

My attendance at the pioneers had not been pleasant, no feeling of euphoria; that, finally, I had been released from alcohol. I was none too sure I had been released from alcohol, and; unlike AA, there had been little talk of drink. You just took a pledge and that was that, that your drinking days were over.

We were to collect our pins the following month, and I thought the whole thing was crazy. It was assumed we, or me; only days off of drink, would still be sober. I had walked out of AA meetings and gone to the nearest pub. It had not troubled me one bit, but this was different if I can't think why, because I did not believe in God. The Sacred Heart. It was all a mumbo-jumbo thing to me, but I did not want to break my oath. All this because I had pissed the bed. But I must admit that the pioneers had been more than friendly. Little wonder. It was rare for them to gain a single new member, but, and suddenly, on a Sunday in September, they had three.

I remember a man named Bill and another Neil and the three ladies who chaired the meeting, Patsy and Pat and Susan. I would later learn that none of them had ever drank much less than drinking to excess. The same was true for almost all of the pioneers, that they knew nothing about drink; except, that is, as they had proven, far better to steer clear of it. After our coffee in Mary's house, I went out for a walk with Davie.

"How do you feel?" he asked.

"I feel like a drink."

"I'm not surprised, but try to hold on – get through today and take tomorrow as it comes."

"It has not been easy so far, to get through today."

"Tomorrow might be better."

"I hope it is."

The following night the doorbell rang and, once again, I was more than pleased that Davie was paying another visit.

That night we must have spoken until two in the morning. I forget about what, the pioneers; his romance that was no more? It would be safe to say that we were both unhappy men. But for all of that it was good to speak to a guy who understood. He understood a lot of things, did Davie. But he is a very private man and it would be unfair to go on at length about him. He had his life and I had mine, if, for a time; during my first weeks as a pioneer, he visited every night. There was always something to speak about and that December we went for a stay in a monastery in Lothian, which is not far from Edinburgh. There were others in the monastery who were recovering from drink or drugs or both and I remember a priest, a man in his seventies, who smoked marihuana.

I had tried marihuana years before, in the sixties; and so, had Davie, but it had done little for either one of us. Not so the priest, who swore by it, that it eased the pain of his rheumatism and lent a feeling of wellbeing. By then, after a very shaky start; and with the help of Davie – I don't know if I could have done it alone, stopped drinking – I had accepted my lot, that I was now a pioneer and no more booze for me.

***

I was on holiday with Rosie on the Spanish island of Majorca when I read of the death of Muhammad Ali in June, 2016. This was a blow to me, the big black man; if he was really more bronze, as a burnished copper, than black. We were staying in the small resort of Porto Christo, which is a quiet place and a far remove from the razzmatazz of Ali's fights. Sonny Liston. Joe Frazier. George Foreman. The list went on and on. Ken Norton and Ernie Shavers, Oscar Bonavena. I remember them all. There are some people who can date a time to a certain song, but for me it was the Ali fights. I was working night shift in the railway when he fought Liston for the second time in Lewiston, Maine, in 1965. This was the first transatlantic fight to be shown live on British television. The satellite that bounced the pictures was named Early Bird. An apt name, because the fight began about three in the morning. There was no way I was for missing this – I thought Liston would win, incidentally – and one of the guys in the shunting yard loaned me his motor bike and I drove it home to watch the fight and then back again when the fight; could you call it that, a fight, was over.

Liston was counted out in the first round, and Ali; he was something then, all gleaming youth, and, as ever, his loud mouth, that Liston was a tramp, a bum, and when I left the house to go back to work, he was still ranting. I felt sorry for Liston, who; in the fight, looked old and stilted; top-heavy, and far too slow for his lithe young foe.

I can think of no heavyweight who would have beaten Ali; the man he was, aged 23, in 1965. But we all age and – ashes to ashes, dust to dust – as the years pass by the fights got tougher, until; in 1980, he was beaten up and stopped in eleven rounds by Larry Holmes in a so-called fight where he had no chance. None at all. And he quit on his stool, which you would never have thought Muhammad to do. The spirit is willing but the flesh is weak. How true! It was never more emphasised than on that night in Las Vegas.

Ali had been just too old; and too many tough fights in

his past, and, to cut it short, had gone to the well one time too many.

But even that was not enough and he fought again, a draw against the limited Trevor Berbick in the Bahamas in 1981. After that he called it quits, but it was far too late and not a happy retirement. Ali had taken a lot of punches; thunderous shots, in his long career and they had to be catching up on him. No man can take the punches he took and stay healthy. That Ali survived; in this world, to the age he was, seventy-four, is a wonder in itself.

Ali was a Black Muslim. A fervent one, by all accounts. Before his fights he had prayed in his corner in a Muslim fashion. The reason he became a Muslim was, I would fancy, because he did not trust white people. Not a bit, and I would doubt if he liked them either. Any white women he went with was kept a guarded secret. A black superman, it is true; but he was also a downright racist that, for some reason – a measure of his charm? – has been overlooked, and he was allowed to carry the torch at the Olympic Games in Atlanta in year 2000. He was a sick man then, fat and flabby and a vacant look, and one thought he might fall as he ran a bit and climbed the steps and lit the Olympic

Flame.

I had Irish grandparents on both sides and they used to say you should not speak ill of the dead, but this amazed me. White America. What shouts of praise and yells of cheer, adulation — it was nothing less — for a man who had despised them. For all of that I had admired Ali hugely. As a boxer. His fights with Frazier and Foreman were amongst the highlights of my life and his death was a blow; as the end of an era, of what should have been the best years of my life.

In Porto Christo I told Rosie I had not thought that his death would have affected me. "Not the way it has."

"Did you ever meet him?"

"No, I never met him; and I never really liked him either — but he was as always around and larger than life when he was young and so was I."

"Do you mean you feel you sort of grew up together?"

I had to laugh at that. "I don't know about Ali, but I think I'm still waiting to grow up." Rosie said she had always thought Ali was a handsome man. "Me and millions of other women."

"And Ali knew it."

"I thought you liked him."

"No, I didn't; but I admired him He always had courage and it is hard sometimes to have courage, to not take the easy way out." I was thinking not of boxing but how, in 1967, Ali had refused to be inducted into the American army. This was the time of the Vietnam war and Ali had said. "No Viet Kong ever called me nigger." It is unlikely he had ever met a Viet Kong to call him nigger, but; because of his stand – and he would have had an easy time in the army – he faced time in jail and was stripped of his title and lost his boxing licence. The real tough, hard fights would come three years later when; and that much older, he was allowed to box again. The old Jewish saying comes back to mind, good luck, bad luck, who knows? For this was the beginning of the end, of epic; almost biblical battles that were too much for any man and all but done for Ali.

Towards the end, in the ring; a clowning Ali – it was about all he could do, clown; shake his head and purse his lips and take the punches and pretend he was not hurt – you wondered what it was all about, that he had come to this.

Rosie knew nothing about boxing, but she knew what boxing had meant to me, and Ali in particular. "You feel sad about this, don't you?"

"I do. He was a great fighter and a man of God."

"I didn't know he was a man of God."

"Of a God as he understood Him."

Rosie said it was much the same. "Not everybody is a Christian."

"Ali wasn't, he believed in Allah."

"He might have been right, who knows?"

"Nobody, and he's not going to come back and tell us, is he?"

"He might be looking down and laughing at us."

"I hope he is."

"But you don't think so?"

"I don't believe in Allah."

"You don't believe in anything."

"That's pretty blunt."

"It is the truth."

"How do you know that?"

"Because I know you."

"I believe in St Jude."

"St Jude believed Jesus was the son of God, so to believe in him you have to believe in Jesus or it makes no sense."

"A lot of things in this world make no sense, and religion is one of them – it is a gift of faith, which Ali had; and I am glad he did, for it would have made his life much easier."

"It might come to you. You should pray to St Jude. One of the mornings you might wake up a man of God, something like Ali was."

"It would be good if I did, and I was almost converted by the Little Flower – you know, St Teresa of Lisieux."

"Then there's hope for you yet."

"I'm still searching."

Rosie said, "I once was lost but now I'm found, you remember that hymn, don't you?"

"Amazing Grace. Of course, I remember it."

"It could happen to you."

"Who knows," I said, "and I hope that Ali is at peace."

***

Should you miss Mass on a Sunday you went to hell. That was the message, loud and clear; and hell was a frightful place. You heard all about it at the missions, that were popular in Glasgow in the fifties. The missionary priests were full of zeal and one night when I was nine or ten years old the priest; a huge man in a brown cassock, said to put your finger above a lighted candle, and, if you thought that sore, to imagine the flames of hell. The whole of you toasting, roasting; burning. It was sufficient to fill me full of fear, too, if nothing else, make sure I was at Mass on Sundays.

The priest went on with a description of hell, which I could have well have done without. Screams and howls and there was no let-up, nor a drop of water either. He was good at his job, that priest; as frightening people up into heaven. The other place was just too awful to contemplate.

303

I remember I was a bit confused and afterwards I asked my father what brimstone was, but I'm not too sure if he knew that himself.

Present day priests seldom, if ever, speak about hell. It is as non-existent. Yet in the Apostles Creed Jesus is said to have descended for three days into hell – the reason for this or has never been explained – before he rose again and ascended into heaven. Seated at the right hand on the Father, who, together with the Holy Ghost, make up the three persons in one God, that, in the Catholic Church, is known as the Holy Trinity.

This, three persons in one God, has confused theologians throughout the ages and you wonder how, and to whom, this information was first imparted.

When my sister Mary imparted it to a Pakistani Muslim he almost collapsed. "Three Gods, never," he exclaimed. "There is only one God and his name in Allah."

Mary insisted there were three. "God the Father and God the Son and the Holy Ghost."

"A ghost?"

"He's really a spirit."

"How can a spirit be a god?"

"That is the mystery of the Holy Trinity."

This conversation was in a shop where Mary was, or had been friendly with the shopkeeper. A man named Salem, who was very devout. "What about Jesus?" he asked her. "I thought that He was the Christian God."

"He is God the Son."

"Who was the wife of the Father?"

"I don't think He had a wife."

"But he had a son?"

Mary said His son was Jesus. "I've already told you, God the Father and God the Son and the Holy Ghost." The Pakistani looked at her like that she was mad. "There is only one God and His name is Allah."

Mary insisted that there were three persons in the Christian god. "They are called the Holy Trinity."

He told her that he had a nephew who was a doctor.

"What do you mean by that?"

Salem put a finger on his temple. "He is a very clever man."

"And you are a very stupid one."

"What did he say to that?"

"He didn't say a single word, but he looked like he would have liked to have wrung my neck."

"He might have thought you were sending him up."

Mary laughed. "He looked astonished."

"Well, it takes a bit of believing – the Holy Trinity, three Gods in one person."

"I thought it a laugh."

"He didn't?"

"Anything but, and then it began to get a bit nasty."

"How, do you mean, nasty?"

"Well, he had suggested that I see a doctor, hadn't he? I was not for taking that and I told him this was a Christian country."

"You did?"

"Why not? Our argument had become quite heated, him and Allah - and I was not going to be browbeaten by a bigot like Salem."

"You could have walked away."

"Why should I have walked away?"

"It would have been easier."

"Not for me, and there's too many people taking the easy way out when it comes to the bit these days. It's high time that Christian's began to stand up for themselves."

I said that it was changing times "Do you remember what that woman in Bolton Abbey said about the Irish, that in the old days wherever they went they took their religion with them. I think it's now something the same with these new immigrants."

Mary said that she thought not. "The Irish were Christians and they went to Christian countries."

"You could get your head cut off for talk like this."

"Do you think I'm scared of Muslim's?"

"No, I'm sure you're not; but you are sounding like a racist."

"You know I'm not a racist. But I get really mad when he suggested I had a hole in the head."

"I think the three persons in one god got to this Salim"

Mary said she was sure they had. "He believes in only one God, Allah, and had never even heard of the Father or Son or the Holy Ghost before I enlightened him."

"I would hardy say enlightened."

"Well, he's heard about them now."

"It'll be the talk of the mosque," I said, "I bet, when he tells his fellow Muslims."

"It's what we believe."

It was?

"You begin mass with it, in the name of the Father and of the Son and the Holy Ghost."

"I think that the Holy Ghost has been changed to the Holy Spirit."

"Not all the time, and it is only because people don't like the word, Ghost."

"I can understand why, and especially if they have children – most children are frightened of ghosts."

Mary said that so was she. "I'd take a fit if I saw one."

"Then I hope you don't."

"So do I!" We were in my house, this on the night of the day she had had words – to say the least – with Salem. "Do you really think it'll be the talk of the mosque, what I told him about the Holy Trinity?"

"I do, and it would have been even better had you told him that we go to hell if we miss Mass on a Sunday."

"It's what they used to say."

"I think it is still the case, only you don't hear too much about hell from priests these days."

"That's because a lot of people would not believe that such a place existed."

"Do you?"

"No."

"But you believe in the Holy Trinity?"

"Not really." Mary smiled. "I suppose I should, but it's a bit much, isn't it?"

***

The Pioneer movement of Total Abstinence was founded by an Irish priest, Father Cullen, in Dublin in

1899. The original idea was for a small, woman-only movement that, by dint of their resolve – not one woman broke her pledge – soon attracted men, who, too, wished to take the pledge of a live of sobriety.

This was well ahead of AA, and it was not meant for problem drinkers who might – slips and worse are common-place in AA – let the movement down. Father Cullen was wise to that and his first members were practically teetotallers This was a measure of necessity, for credibility; that Pioneers were sober people.

When I first joined, I was on probation, because you had to be off of drink for two years before you could become a full member. I think the probationary period has now dropped to one year, not that it matters very much, one year or ten; for, for the alcoholic, one day can be a long, long time and that is why I omitted to mention that, initially, I had taken an oath for only two years. Only? It is easy to say now, only; when, at the time, it was more hour by hour. The Librium helped, but after a while I quit on them and was as thrown back on myself.

Now and again some-one might ask what my little

badge meant and, for I was fed up with the whole shebang, I would tell them it was none of their business. That was the man I was. A no-nonsense guy when I was sober and I was always sober, so they had to wonder about that one too. My strange life. I had gone from one extreme to yet another, but it was not the Pioneers that kept me sober, no; more, what I have said before, I had hit rock bottom when I peed the bed and I did not want to drink again. Yet, too, as time went on and I recovered, it was good to be a Pioneer and I was not slow with that information whenever I was in drinking company. I had come a long hard road with many knocks and, wherever I was; in whatever situation, alcohol was not for me and, truthfully, for many years, it has been the last thing on my mind.

***

On the writing front I had nothing published for twelve years. This was more than dismal, especially when I had completed two novels but could not find a publisher. Not that two novels in twelve years is much to brag about, but a lot of work had gone into them and it was depressing that my efforts had come to nothing. Part of my problem was that I wanted to write a classic, when, and in what I considered to be my best work, *it might Have been Jerusalem*, I had come closer to a comic horror story. This was a try to raise the roof, to be different from most other writers, if, that was, for my efforts were on and off and mostly off, I could call myself a writer. I sometimes wondered why I cared, and it could not have been for money. I had made a few thousand from my boxing book, A *Hurting Business*, but that had gone on drink. Ten years later I had my biggest hit with *I Have heard you Calling in the Night*. This was serialised by *The Mail on Sunday* and was published in America and the Italian translation was something of a best seller. It cleared my debts and I had the freedom to travel, but, still, to maintain a decent life style, I was dependent on grants and bursaries when I would have much preferred to have been a self-supporting writer. Then again, something like my own life, my style was all at odds and a far remove from more calculating, as formative; tell-a-story writers. I was more in the mould, and especially with It might Have been Jerusalem, of the American short story writer, Charles Bukowski, who, I'm sure, had endured his share of hardship, of being ignored. Another fault, flaw of mine —

could you call it that, a flaw – I was not the best at playing up to the literary big-wigs down in London.

***

Mary asked if I any plans for late November and when I said no, I hadn't, I was told about a pilgrimage that was going to Guadalupe in Mexico where, so I had heard amongst the faithful, Our Lady had appeared to a peasant named Juan Diego in 1531. "There's a direct flight from London to Mexico City." This was July and November seemed far, far away; but time goes in – there is no stopping it, time – and November came and we flew to London and joined with our group in Heathrow airport and went through customs and on to the plane and Mary said: "You get around as a pilgrim, don't you?"

Writing this and looking back, all down the years, I am astonished; and forget the booze, at all the mistakes that I have made. My father's death and the age I was is some excuse, that for a time I became a shipbreaker. There was excitement in this, but it was all small, petty stuff and the phase – that was all it was, a phase - passed over, but not before, as I have said before, I had spent some time in a detention pitch where a good half of the staff were child molesters. This, in that place; it was named Larchgrove, was, those perverted men, the first I began to appreciate the qualities of my father. He had been an upright man and a man of God and I remember wishing that he was with me there, in Larchgrove. I would have felt a whole lot safer, and that's a fact.

It was not long after Larchgrove that I acquired an interest in boxing. This was to be no passing thing, no; rather, as time went on, an almost damn obsession. But I proceed too quickly and should explain that as a boy my one true talent was playing football. With a bit of encouragement, I honestly feel I could have made the grade and, possibly, have played for Glasgow Celtic. At the time it had been my fond hope, and I was crazy about football until my father – not that he cared about the football, and would have much preferred had I had been an altar boy – died and I lost interest. Why? I have often wondered, pondered that one and I can only think that I did not want the sympathy of the other boys in the football sides I played for.

It was my first mistake, the football; my quitting it, for, for all my fascination, I was no good as a boxer. Not that I tried too hard to become a boxer, but, when I was fifteen, I had a pal of sorts named John O'Brian who was a professional fighter, and a good one, too. He would go on to fight for the British featherweight title. A problem for O'Brian, he was very much a street guy. It was how I got to know him, hanging around the corners. We became quite close and I ended up in his boxing gym. His trainer was a man named Jim Stevenson who soon had me skipping rope and punching bags and I was advised to go for a five-mile run first thing in the morning. I missed out on that one, and I think that O'Brian did too. He was not the most committed of boxers, John O'Brian. But I liked the guy, who was a plumber to trade. I remember we had a leaking tap and came up to the house and sorted it. Eventually, when he thought I was fit enough, Stevenson had me in the ring for a sparring session with a guy who was three years older and two stone heavier than I was. We wore big, heavy; almost clumsy gloves, and after a minute or so I was hit on the chest, under my heart. The pain was shocking and I had not thought you could be hit so hard and

Stevenson saw that I was hurt and stopped the session immediately.

I lost a lot of my enthusiasm for boxing that night, after that punch; and if I went back to the gym a couple more times, I made sure I was not sparring – not with a guy who was three years older and two stones heavier, anyhow. It turned out that I never sparred again. I was too busy chasing money and chasing girls to pause to train, to become a boxer. That and, the punch I took had sickened me of boxing, as a boxer, if, at the time, I was loath to admit it, even to myself. And you must admit things to yourself or you are living in a fairyland, and I was to live in fairylands for a good part of my life. In the railway, when; had I the wits of a goose, I could have been a well-doing young man. The pay was good and there had been no need for me to steal. We were not bad off, my mother and sister and me, for, at that time, all of us were working. My mother as a dining lady in local schools and Mary in offices and, latterly, as a traffic warden. As for me, as said before, I was in a fairyland, always looking but never finding. What? The peace of death, if death is peace; but even that was not to be. I was full of energy and a robust good health, but had no sense.

A stay in a monastery at that time would have done me a world of good. But rather than that I went to London, and on from there to Europe. A wild trip, but everything was wild and it would stay that way until I came by Martin. It is strange what a dog can do, as stabilise a man. What Martin did for me. I was his sole support, and supporting him I had to take care of myself. Had I gone to prison it would have done for him, so I lived a much more peaceful life and I began to change. With my mother. We went to midnight mass on Christmas Eve for eight years running. I even became friends with the parish priest, Father O'Hagan. This was the first I had been inside a chapel for almost thirty years and I was surprised to discover that the mass had been changed from my boyhood Latin into English. Not that it mattered and a good feeling; with my mother in the crowded well-lit chapel in, outside, the cold bleak winter night. When we came home, I would go out again with Martin. A walk around a near-by field where I would think about the mass and the priests – there were three priests on the altar on Christmas Eve – and a common bond that we, the priests and me, all were bachelors.

This, that I was a single man, did not escape the attention of Father O'Hagan, who, to my huge surprise, offered the hint that I was still young enough for a late vocation. The idea was preposterous and how Father O'Hagan came up with that one I will never know. But strange things happen and I had been in some strange places, if never yet in a seminary. That aside, Father O'Hagan was a good man and it was a privilege to have known him.

Along with midnight mass on Christmas Eve I accompanied my mother on saints' days and Evening Devotions and Station of the Cross. I was never there on a Sunday, though; which makes Father O'Hagan's hint to the priesthood all the stranger. But I enjoyed my visits and I knew my mother liked to have me there, beside her in the chapel. On Mary's suggestion we; all three, with Martin in the lead – he liked his novena, Martin did - made numerous visits to a Tuesday night novena to St Anthony in St Francis in the Gorbals. It got that Martin, when I said St Anthony; began to leap and bark in sheer delight.

The strange thing is that Martin and St Anthony seem now to be much further back than when I was a schoolboy. I was in my forties, so I can't think why; but it is a fact; writing now, looking back. Our nights at the novena. We sat at the rear and not once, during all out nights in St Francis, did Martin cause the slightest trouble. I sometimes thought I had a big mouse with me, and he was far from that; mouse-like. But without him, his arrival in the house, there was not a hope I would have been in the chapel, the Tuesday night novenas. The chances are I would have been drunk, if, that was, I had not been murdered. It is easy to be murdered in any city but it was particularly so in Glasgow in the eighties – and it still might be for all I know – to be maimed or murdered, done in, in the local parlance.

This is passing, but it is very true; the violence that is, or was, in Glasgow. I had had a brick in my face when I was ten years old and was lucky not to have lost an eye. In the years to come I was even more lucky that I did not lose my life.

It was good to be away from that, or as far away as one could be away from it if you lived in the inner city. This is a frightful truth; and Glasgow is, undoubtedly, the city of the scar.

On our way to the novena, we passed by my old school, St Bonaventures. They had night-time activities and there were usually groups of youths loitering outside the building. Martin usually growled at them, but they took it in good part. What else? He was big by then and not a dog to mess with. We must have passed by the school at least ten times and there was no trouble. Then one particular Tuesday the place exploded. A gang rumble between some twenty or thirty youths. There were buckets of blood, for they fought with weapons, axes and knifes and I saw one boy have his face sliced open with an open razor. There was nothing I could do. Not a thing. I had Martin, but even without Martin there was nothing much I could have done, and I was not for hanging around for the cops to come and want me for a witness. Nor was Mary, for that matter. She was too wise to the ways of the street for that one. But it ruined the night, and, as on a blink, a razor glint, yet more young blood on Glasgow's streets.

I had discovered a better way of life, with animals. My dog, Martin. His needs were simple, and a total trust and loyalty. My new world of parks and empty spaces was a much more gentle, peaceful place than life amongst the humans. It is rare for a dog to want to maim or kill amongst their kind without the encouragement of humans. The barbarous sort who turns a dog against its nature. Dog is God spelled backwards and Martin loved the novena to St Anthony. So, did I. In my way. The preacher was a Father Noel, and his sermons were good and I liked the hymns; that, some of them, were sung in Latin. It has a particular charm, Latin in the Catholic Church, or, perhaps, it is a harp back to my childhood.

This new, as different me since I had acquired Martin. I was not the bold drunkard I had been before, but rather sleeked; in the house, if, sometimes, as is the way with drink, I went out and ended up in trouble. Nothing serious, a couple of nights at most in jail. This over a ten-year span, so it was hardly living dangerously. I was walking, sometimes, ten or fifteen miles a day and keeping mostly to myself. A time for thought, reflection; for I was now at an age where I had a past but was still young enough to have a future. There was the occasional woman, who was usually married. Not that I cared, and; if I am honest, a married woman is less hassle than a single one. Provided you are not caught, that is; and I was never caught. Found out. A man of books – I was never away from the library – and the open road, and an attender at the chapel. There was a sort of solace in the chapel, which puzzled me; for I could not believe in the Catholic, or Christian faith. It came over to me as a man-made thing, not that I would say as much to any of the faithful. A little deceit is neither here nor there if it does no harm. I was now going to mass on Sunday mass with my mother; who, I'm sure, hoped that I might see the light. I hoped it too; that, as some blinding flash, I was finally converted.

It was not to happen, for all I tried – and I did try – to make sense of what through all the ages has remained a mystery. St Michael, the Archangel; Lucifer's revolt in heaven, but how did mortals know all this, in; as it must have been, a time before creation?

The three persons in one God that Mary had argued with the Muslim about was yet another, but good for her that she is blessed with faith for, from what I have seen, it makes for a happier state of mind.

In regard to my own lack of faith I was concerned

enough to approach Father O'Hagan who sympathised and said that he would pray for me. "It might happen yet, that you become a true believer."

I doubted it, and how; if God was all powerful, had Satin all but toppled Him in Heaven long ago?

It had been a close thing, so it is claimed – but claimed by whom? – before Lucifer; who had suffered from the sin of pride, was finally subdued and chained in hell forever.

Father O'Hagan advised me not to think but to accept. "The Lord works in mysterious ways."

I agreed. He certainly did. A bit of faith. Blessed are those who believe without having seen me. I wished that I was one of them. Shoulder to shoulder with Father O'Hagan fighting the good fight. That when I died I would, to use a phrase, go to glory

"It's what they say in the Salvation Army," I said to Mary on the plane, on our flight to Mexico. "I very nearly became a member."

"I didn't know that."

"It's a long story, but I used to go to a service in the Salvation Army almost every Sunday night."

"Was this in Glasgow?"

"It was. And they were good people, but I was drinking heavily at the time so you can guess what happened."

"You were flung out?"

"What else? They frown on drink and a drunk man in the congregation is something they can do without."

"This is all news to me."

"I suppose it is, but I don't tell you everything."

We had been speaking about the funeral rite of a mutual acquaintance, a non-Catholic who had recently passed. "Why were you in the Salvation Army?"

"I knew a girl who was a member, and it went from there."

"Then you must have been sober, to begin with, anyhow."

"I was. Not a drop. It went on for a while and I think she thought I was a proper gentleman."

"I'm sure she did."

"But then I got drunk, and I wasn't a gentleman

anymore."

"That must have come as shock to her, the man you really were."

"It did. She was shamed. And so, I, for that matter." By then I has met her parents who were good, respectable people who thought that I was a good, respectable man. It is a painful memory, for I had really liked their daughter. But it must be that I liked drink more, for at one of the Sunday services I very drunk. A few curse words and a struggle with a couple of male Army members who tried to throw me out. It was a winter night and snow on the ground and, drunk as I was, I wondered if I could repent – or win back my girlfriend, more to the point – and with that in mind, a plea for forgiveness, I rejoined the already disturbed service. I was again ejected, and the police were called and, really, the whole thing was a horror.

"Her name was Julie, and I really, really liked her."

"But not enough to stop you drinking."

"It was more a lapse."

"Lapse or not it cost you dearly, if you liked this Julie the way you're telling me."

"I think I liked her even more than I'm telling you."

"How long ago was all of this?"

"Long enough for her to be a grandmother now or even gone to Glory, if I hope she's not; gone to Glory."

Mary said so did she. "It sounds like she was a nice person."

"She was."

"But you blew it."

"I've blown practically everything in my entire life."

"But you're still here, and soon you'll be in Mexico."

"Do you remember our first pilgrimage, to St Jude's in the Black Forrest?"

Mary said she did. "I think you fancied Monika."

"She was an attractive woman."

Mary laughed. "You mewed like a cat and she brought you a glass of milk"

"That goes to show she was kindly, too."

"It was dead funny, I thought."

"So did I."

"It was our first pilgrimage together."

"I loved the chapel to St Jude," I said. "Do you remember the letter I read in Spanish? It had a huge effect on me."

"I know it had."

"It was my introduction to St Jude, in that little chapel. There was something there that was almost supernatural. All my troubles had just gone away and I could not believe it.

"I had almost forgotten what peace was like until I was in that chapel."

Mary said I was an unusual pilgrim and St Jude might have put in an extra effort. "I mean, you've been back to visit him a few times since."

"I have, and I intend to visit him a few times more."

"A few more pilgrimages."

"Sure," I said, "why not? I like a pilgrimage and the modern pilgrim has a life of Riley."

"Do you know who Riley was?"

"I haven't a clue."

"Neither have I, but you often hear it – if people are having an easy time."

"I hope we have an easy time in Mexico."

In the air, on the plane – it was big and had lots of passengers – Mary said that I should write about our pilgrimages.

"I don't know if I could."

"I think you could."

"It would be a very strange book."

"Some people like to read strange books."

"It's years since I have written anything."

"Then It could be a new beginning."

Printed in Great Britain
by Amazon

39440195R00188